FATHER
YOUR-
SELF
FIRST

Annotations around the lettering: ADVENTURE · BECOMING! · 1" · *LEGACY · ENGAGING · EXPECTA...

ADVENTURE

FATHER YOUR-SELF FIRST

BECOMING!

LEGACY

ENGAGING

EXPECTATIONS

**EVERYTHING YOU NEED TO BECOME
THE FATHER YOUR FAMILY DESERVES**

GLEN HENRY

NELSON
BOOKS

An Imprint of Thomas Nelson

Published by Nelson Books, an imprint of Thomas Nelson, 501 Nelson Place, Nashville, TN 37214, USA. Nelson Books and Thomas Nelson are registered trademarks of HarperCollins Christian Publishing, Inc.

Published in association with Yates & Yates, www.yates2.com.

Thomas Nelson titles may be purchased in bulk for educational, business, fundraising, or sales promotional use. For information, please email SpecialMarkets@ThomasNelson.com.

ISBN 978-1-4002-5398-2 (ePub)
ISBN 978-1-4002-5255-8 (HC)

HarperCollins Publishers, Macken House, 39/40 Mayor Street Upper, Dublin 1, D01 C9W8, Ireland (https://www.harpercollins.com)

Library of Congress Control Number: 2025014571

Printed in the United States of America
25 26 27 28 29 LBC 5 4 3 2 1

Dedicated to the Chocolate Babies:
Theo P, Uriah Beau, Anaya Zai, and Uzi;
to my incredibly beautiful and patient wife, Yvette;
and to all the men who have held me
accountable—don't stop!

CONTENTS

Introduction

I NEVER WANTED TO BE A FATHER

Start

When I was growing up, I never wanted to be a father. Bringing kids into this world seemed inconvenient, even irresponsible. I couldn't imagine myself ever having kids or being a dad.

That seems ironic considering my career today is based on showing people the truth about fatherhood, but it makes sense if you know about the way I grew up. My parents had me as teenagers—my mom was sixteen and my dad, nineteen—and were not in a committed relationship. Nineteen was an interesting age in Baltimore, Maryland. Living in a rough neighborhood, being an immigrant, and having no direction mixed with that age left my dad open to a certain kind influence from the streets. A lot of his friends died or went to jail, and he didn't have only me to think about. My dad had a choice to make: stay in Baltimore with his son and tough it out in the streets or move to San Diego with his expectant fiancée and start over. I'm sure the decision wasn't easy, and from what I understand, the plan was to take me with him. But I ended up in Maryland with my mom, and my dad moved to San Diego with my soon-to-be stepmom, Sherry, where they had my little sister, Britni.

Though those events happened forty years ago, they have shaped my life in ways I'm still unpacking. My dad made the right decision for him; in a sense I'd say he fathered himself through that choice. But leaving me with my mom meant I was without the daily guidance a young man needs from his father.

I would visit California every summer after I turned five years old. I had to adapt to the push and pull of plane rides back and forth with chaperones and learning the rules of two homes, like being fairly independent in one home and limited in another. The ripple effects of bicoastal, multicultural joint custody created a level of code switching that should be studied. However, the message was clear: Kids are inconvenient. My mom and dad's parenting—both the presence of it and the lack of it, the good of it and the bad of it—affected me deeply. That's not an accusation or an excuse, but simply a reality—a reality that every child experiences and one that follows them into adulthood.

My mom had a few long-term relationships but never married. When I was nine, my brother, Blease, was born. As I entered my preteen years and began to look more like a man instead of a little boy, my mom's treatment of me seemed to grow more intense, for whatever reason. Maybe in her mind she was trying to "correct" or "teach" me, but I remember lines often being crossed. At the time, I recall wishing I had a father present in the home who could help parent me. I love my mom deeply, and I understand it's tough to be a single parent. But the reality is that those years and experiences were deeply damaging to my inner child and to my concept of fatherhood, and it's a big part of the reason why I'm so passionate about fatherhood and family today.

For example, tensions were often high around my house. Everyone, me included, seemed to be defensive and on edge all the time. My mom was always yelling about something. By the time I was a teenager, I couldn't wait to get out of the house—and I definitely never wanted to be a father.

I started wilding. Tripping. I got kicked out of the house a lot, and I'd go sleep at my aunt's place or my grandmother's. I finally left home at seventeen and went to live with my grandmother in her one-bedroom apartment. A year later, my mom and Blease moved into my grandmother's place too, so I went to live with my aunt. That didn't last long either. After that I moved in with my girlfriend and her family.

By age twenty, I wasn't in a good place mentally or emotionally. I remember calling my dad and telling him I was planning to kill myself. He started crying on the phone. He asked me to fly out to where he lived in Escondido, California, so on August 31, 2005, I moved in with my dad.

In California, my life slowly got more stable. I loved hip-hop, which I had been introduced to early on by Uncle Jahson, my stepmother's brother. So I took a job as a roadie for Thoughts Aloud, a local hip-hop group. I didn't love the job, but I started to enjoy being part of something. That would eventually lead me into a career as a hip-hop artist, including recording several albums and going on countless tours.

I grew up attending church a few times a year, but in California, a childhood friend of mine named Garrett invited me to his church. Soon I began going regularly. My faith became (and remains) a vital part of my life.

That church is where I met the person primarily responsible for changing my view of fatherhood. His name was Patrick Lynch, but we all called him Pat. He was the high school pastor. I'll talk more about Pat and a few other mentors later on, but for now I'll just say he was the person who helped me believe in fatherhood. There wasn't any one moment or conversation that flipped a switch in me. It was mostly just seeing fatherhood modeled in a way I had never experienced before. Pat's home was proof that family could work. I was amazed by the peace, by the way they got along, and by how welcoming their home felt. Suddenly I saw what family could look like, and for the first time ever, I could see myself in the role of a father.

A couple of years later, I met my wife, Yvette. We got married in 2010, and two and a half years after that, our son Theo was born. Whether I was ready for it or not, I was now a father.

Today, I can honestly say I love fatherhood. I don't love certain parts of it—such as the whining, the battles over eating vegetables, and all the parts having to do with bodily functions and odors—but I realize now I was born to be a father, called to be a father, and blessed to be a father. Fatherhood has changed my life, and I've watched it do the same for many other men. I've come to see the incredible power it holds not just to shape, serve, and bless our children but to create a better world.

PROVING GREAT FATHERS EXIST

Sometimes people use the word *example* to describe my family, and I hate it. I literally have a physical reaction to that word because it's the opposite of what I believe myself to be. I'm not an example for anyone to imitate, and I can't tell you how to live or what to do. I'm not you, and I'm not parenting your kids. Instead of an example, I want to be *proof* that fatherhood works. That's why the tagline of my organization is "Proving great fathers exist, one day at a time."

This book is part of that goal, but it goes beyond it: I am inviting you to be part of the process. Your family can be proof of fatherhood for other people to be inspired and encouraged by.

I believe there are a lot of strong families out there, but they're not necessarily accessible to people. Instead, whether on the news or in the gossip rounds, we mostly hear about dysfunction: who got divorced, who cheated on whom, who walked out on their family. I'm not shaming anyone who has experienced those things, but if we can so easily listen to and repeat the negative things, we should also be able to repeat the positive things. We should be willing to let the beauty of family and fatherhood shine.

If you don't think you fit the "ideal" definition of a father, that's okay. Honestly, none of us fits it because we all have our quirks, traumas, weaknesses, and mistakes. For the love of our kids, though, we need to be willing to step into our roles and grow into the fathers we're created to be. You might be a single father. You might be an experienced father, a first-time father, or an expectant father. You might be divorced and sharing custody of your children. You might be a grandparent or an uncle who has a close relationship with kids who need a father figure. You might be a spiritual father or a mentor to other people. All those roles are not only valid, they're vital. So while I'm going to speak from my very unique experience as a married, Black father of four who lives on a farm in the California desert, works from home as a content creator, and homeschools his kids, I hope you can find a lot here that speaks to *you*.

Let me emphasize that I'm going to speak from my experience as a father—but that in no way implies motherhood is less important! I could not do what I do without Yvette. I honor her, respect her, and love her beyond what I can put into words. Much of what I'll say in these pages applies equally to mothers and fathers, but this book is about fatherhood, so please don't get upset when I don't qualify everything I say by adding "and mothers too!" That's a given.

Also, if I can be so bold: Please don't get offended on behalf of our children. We take our responsibility to protect them incredibly seriously. They appear on my channel all the time, but they are not forced to participate, and they enjoy it. We have regular family consent meetings where we make sure they are okay with how they're being portrayed. They also earn money from the videos, which is both a great opportunity for them and really good training.

I remember Yvette asking me once, "Is this a family business, or is our family a business?" At first I was like, "Who cares? What's the difference?" But then I stopped and thought about it. Our family is not for sale. While we have built a business based on the family we are blessed to parent, the family comes first—not the business. This never became clearer to us than a couple of years ago when Theo asked me to take down the videos he was in because he wasn't comfortable with people knowing so much about him. I removed seven hundred videos. It was a significant hit to our income, to the point we had to sell our house. But now he's realizing the power of storytelling to build his own future, and he's comfortable appearing in the videos again. Without question, though, our kids come first, and they always will.

The word BELEAF, which I'm using as an acronym to structure this book, is my rap moniker as well as the name of our organization, Beleaf in Fatherhood. I chose the name Be*leaf* rather than Be*lief* because I'm passionate about authenticity and honesty—and there's no *lie* in what I'm saying. Because of that passion, I'm not going to sugarcoat fatherhood in this book. As I'm sure you've already discovered, carrying out this role is going to cost you a lot of money, and your furniture will have some dents in it, and your car will be full of sand and crumbs, and at times you'll be creeped out by tiny humans staring at you when you wake up.

It's worth it though. Your kids need to *experience* great fatherhood, and society needs *proof* of great fatherhood.

WELCOME BLACK

While I'm not only writing *for* Black men, I am writing *as* a Black man. I have a deep desire to see Black men and Black families become visible proof of the power of family. That's why I start many of my videos with the phrase "Welcome Black." I want to embrace the value of my identity and inspire others to do the same.

A while back a friend I've known for years, a white guy, came up to me at church and said, "Thank you for posting all those videos. It gives us a window into your family. I didn't know how you guys lived."

That last phrase was so weird to me. What did he mean he didn't know how we lived? Did he think we were eating our children? Practicing voodoo? It almost made me mad. But it also reminded me that a lot of people don't know what we (Black families) are like because they haven't seen very many.

One of the problems is that other people have been telling our story for too long, but it's the wrong story. It's the story of the absent Black father, the angry Black man, the broken Black family. If you look back over history, this narrative is not new, and it often feels intentional.

Consider slavery in America. Enslaved people were not allowed to marry, and if they did so secretly, they were often separated. Any children from their union were the legal property of their parents' owners and were frequently taken from one or both parents. The "right" of slave owners to sell off individual family members was enshrined in law in the infamous Slave Codes. Why would they do that? I think that in large part, it was because slave owners were afraid of the power of family. They didn't want families growing and multiplying, because they would become strong.

Think about that for a moment. If Black families were such a threat that slave owners intentionally fragmented them, how much power could a family have in society today? How much strength could *your* home and *my* home provide for a society that desperately needs a new narrative around fatherhood, especially Black fatherhood? There is power inherent in our families—power not just to change our own future but to change the lives of those around us and even society itself.

Slavery was abolished long ago, but even today, forces still target Black families. Think about the War on Drugs, which disproportionately affected Black men and damaged countless families. Think about redlining and other housing and education policies that made it more difficult for Black families to prosper. Think about massacres that targeted Black businesses and destroyed generational wealth, such as the Tulsa Race Massacre. Think about police brutality toward Black people, including young boys and teenagers. Think about how often and how loudly news outlets broadcast the crimes of Black men and tell society we are to be feared and controlled, not loved or trusted. Think about politicians who dehumanize us, who propagate stereotypes, and who rely on fearmongering to gain political clout.

The sad reality is that in America, many people have a built-in, subconscious fear of Black people. I have Black children, and I cannot sleep well at night knowing that people are going to fear my kids and view them as threats. I will fight to change that narrative. We *all* must fight to change it.

History and current statistics point to a harsh reality: Black men—and Black fathers, in particular—are often working from a deficit. We're playing from behind, and we have one arm tied behind our backs. Society breaks our families apart, then blames us for being broken, and finally uses our brokenness as an excuse to break us even more. If we stay silent, the injustice continues; if we speak up, we're labeled whiners or agitators. It often feels like a lose-lose.

Don't get me wrong: I'm not playing the victim here. I'm proud of the strength of Black people, and I believe with all my heart that the future is ours to step into with faith and courage. But I'm also very aware of the systemic, systematic attacks on Black fatherhood, and I'm pissed off.

The first time my family videos went viral, you should have seen all the racist comments people made about me: "The monkeys are multiplying," "He'll be gone in two weeks," and other stuff like that. At first I was sad about it. Then I got mad. I wanted to find their IP addresses and punch them in the face. But eventually I realized that many people actually believe these things because, as I said earlier, *they haven't seen anything else.*

Our family together represents way more than just a cute family who loves each other on YouTube. It represents more than just the importance of fatherhood. We are working hard to reclaim an image that has been twisted and hidden by society. We can't legislate fear and false narratives out of people's hearts. Instead, we must show the world something different. We have to live a different truth: *our* truth.

I know this, and you know this, but the world needs to know it: *Black families are beautiful.* We live with contagious passion. We work hard, play hard, and laugh hard. Our culture is as strong as it is diverse. We are deeply angry at injustice, but we're also fiercely proud of our resilience. We are unashamed, unstoppable, and invaluable. We don't have to prove anything to anybody, but our very lives and families *are* proof—proof that Black families are not only possible but also a gift to the world.

This goes beyond Black people, of course. False stories are being told about Christian families, Muslim families, Hispanic families, single-parent families, same-sex parent families, white families. It's not your responsibility to change everybody's perspective, but if that story is not true—if a lie is being told about you—then the best way to reclaim your story is to live it out, loud and proud, and let the haters and the critics be silenced by your presence.

You can't control what other people think or say about you, but you can choose the family you're going to be. Even if your own family background is less than ideal, you have the power to make changes with God's grace. You can learn and grow. You can write a different story and build a better future.

And it starts with having a *beleaf* in fatherhood.

Part Number

BECOMING

Title

Start

In a technical sense, you became a father the day you did your part to conceive a baby. But that's only the beginning because your kids need more than a biological father. They need someone who knows them, cares for them, stays with them, protects them, trains them, and serves them.

These are skills you learn over time, through effort and experience. In other words, you *become* the father your kids need and deserve. Fatherhood is a role you grow into, and without a doubt, it's the most transformative role you will ever have. It will expand you, teach you, test you, and bless you. (It will also drain you, strain you, stress you, and distress you at times, but let's not focus on that!)

The choice to grow into better versions of ourselves is something each of us must embrace on our own. In **chapter 1, "Father Yourself First,"** we talk about the importance of taking responsibility for how we show up as fathers. This is about self-reflection, healing, and growth.

Besides internal growth and self-healing, we also need to become more skilled at the day-to-day art of parenting our individual kids. In **chapter 2, "An Expert on Your Children,"** we look at the uniqueness of each child and the value in studying them and learning about them, especially as they grow and change over time.

Chapter Number

FATHER YOURSELF FIRST

Title

Start

Whenever my wife packs our bags for a flight somewhere, I get nervous. It's not because she doesn't do a good job packing. She packs for herself and all the kids, and she remembers everything—medicine, snacks, hygiene bags, shower caps, water shoes, and even extra shoelaces. The problem is that when we get to the counter at the airport, I know at least one of our bags will be overweight. Even though we weigh our luggage before we leave, somehow that bag is going to gain half a pound in the car.

The process that follows makes my skin crawl. I feel my breathing getting shallow just thinking about it. As the airline worker stands at the counter judging me, and as the line behind us grows longer and angrier, I have to open the suitcase and use my mental scale to figure out what articles might add up to half a pound.

When our luggage is wide open and I'm hunched over it trying to figure out what is necessary and what can be thrown away, I find the craziest stuff in there. Stuff I had no idea we were carrying around with us and stuff that doesn't belong in our bags at all. It's just dead weight.

I've realized that, in the same way, I have stuff packed away inside me that I'm unaware of—certain things hurting my marriage, my kids, and me, but I drag them along, year after year, because I haven't fully examined the contents of the bag that is my heart. When it comes to the inner me, I'm still trying to unpack what I'm carrying from my childhood and teen years: the bully in my head, fear of failure, fear of rejection, perfectionism, a hot temper, and more. Life put those things into me, but I never took them out. And now they show up in how I treat my family, how I handle problems, and how I talk to myself.

It gets crazier. Sometimes I'm carrying around other people's bags, and I don't even realize it. Some traumas and troubles in my family history never got dealt with, so they got passed on to me. I've got armfuls of frayed luggage full of someone else's dirty laundry that is weighing me down and tripping me up, and I've never stopped to say, "What in the world am I carrying? Who packed this? Why am I dealing with it, not them? Do I even want this anymore?" I'm not blaming anyone else for my issues. I'm just saying that many of the things I carry are not there because I chose to have them but because I didn't choose to leave them behind. *And that's on me now.* It doesn't matter who packed my bags. I am responsible for examining my own life and figuring out what is going on with my own self. I have to check myself, repack myself, and take responsibility for myself.

I have to father myself.

> **MANY OF THE THINGS I CARRY ARE NOT THERE BECAUSE I CHOSE TO HAVE THEM BUT BECAUSE I DIDN'T CHOOSE TO LEAVE THEM BEHIND.**

THE "BEST YOU CAN DO" SHOULD KEEP GETTING BETTER

Fathering yourself means taking on the role of father for your own life. You treat yourself the way a responsible, healthy father would treat their child. This is about owning who you are right now *in order to grow into a healthier person in the future*—just like parents do for their kids when they're young. I don't know what your father did or didn't do for you, but I know what you can do for you:

- You can teach yourself.
- You can correct yourself.
- You can protect yourself.
- You can love yourself.
- You can show yourself compassion.
- You can believe in yourself.
- You can encourage yourself.
- You can hold yourself accountable.

Those are just a few of the things a father should do, right? I'll bet you're doing these things for your kids right now because they come naturally when you truly love your children and are involved in their lives. But do you do them for *you*?

I was talking with my therapist some time ago, and he said something that left me shook. "Glen, how come you're so much better at encouraging your kids than you are at encouraging yourself?"

That question stayed in my mind for weeks. Heck, I'm still thinking about it because it's true. I know what my kids need, and I'll do anything to give it to them. But I suck at doing those things for *me*.

I can't afford not to do those things though. Neither can you. Even if we didn't have someone to teach, correct, protect, or encourage us, we can't parent from that place of deficiency. We'll only reproduce our own lack and our own pain.

A while back I was speaking with my mom about some of the things that messed me up as a kid. She got defensive. She told me, "I did the best I could. I'm not going to apologize for what I didn't know back then."

That made me so mad. Now, since that conversation, she's started going to therapy, and she's taking steps forward, which is great. But at that moment, I was pissed. *Why can't you apologize?* I was thinking. *You're not perfect. Can't you see that?*

Notice what she said: "I did the best I could" and "I'm not going to apologize." Those are two different things, and it's important to separate them. Okay, she was doing the best she could. I'll give her that. After all, *her* mom struggled with substance abuse. It's okay for her to have compassion on that past version of herself, and I'll have compassion too.

But the reality is that her past version hurt me deeply. That person made mistakes throughout my adolescence and teen years that left a legacy of trauma I'm still unpacking. That person might not be today's person, but today's person can still own up for what that person did.

Do you follow? Saying "I did the best I could" doesn't magically erase the pain of the mistakes you make, excuse you from saying you're sorry, or give you permission to stay the same.

Real talk, in ten years I'm sure I'll have to apologize to my kids for some of the things I'm doing today as a dad. I don't know what they are because I'm figuring this dad thing out as I go, just like all of us. So I can't let fear of mistakes keep me from stepping into my role as father, but I also can't throw up my hands and claim, "This is the best I can do" just to avoid confronting the pain my mistakes may cause my kids. I just have to keep showing up every day, willing to work and willing to learn.

I've seen two wrong reactions when men who were raised in dysfunctional environments become fathers. One is to say, "I'm just messed up, yo. I've got problems that can't be fixed. I'm doing the best I can, so if that's not enough, too bad." The other reaction is the opposite extreme: "I'm going to be perfect. I'm going to give my kids everything I wanted and never had."

The first reaction is resignation. They're allowing themselves to keep carrying things that are harmful to them and their families. Instead of taking time to sort through the baggage they've accumulated along the way, they've accepted their current state as if it were a life sentence.

The second reaction I described above is perfectionism. Some people put pressure on themselves that God himself is not putting on them, and they hold themselves to an impossible standard. The problem, of course, is that they can end up spoiling their kids when they should be training them. They'll let them get away with things that actually hurt them because they are unwilling to be the bad guy.

Both resignation and perfectionism are reactions, and reactionary living is not a great success strategy. Rather than reacting, start fathering yourself. Yes, you might be dealing with some issues, but they're not insurmountable. You have wounds, but they're not incurable. You didn't have the parents you needed then, but you can become the parent you need now. Not just for your kids—for yourself. Do the best you can today, but continue to father yourself so "the best you can do" keeps getting better until it's the very best it can be.

BE THE RIGHT VOICE IN YOUR HEAD

As we saw above, fathering yourself means taking ownership of who you are: your traumas, your mindsets, your habits, your character. You have to keep teaching and training yourself throughout your life rather than carrying around bags full of stuff you don't want.

There's another aspect of this that is equally important: fathering yourself through difficult situations. This is about being your own encourager and motivator. Too often, we have a voice in our heads that is literally abusive. We become our own bullies, our worst critics, our biggest haters.

Because my career is to make videos about my family, I can go back and watch my parenting style like a coach breaking down game film. Recently I was studying some old footage, and as I watched myself dealing with my kids' malfunctions, I noticed how much grace I was showing them.

Then I heard a voice in my head, as if I knew exactly what my therapist would ask. *Glen, why aren't you giving yourself the same grace as you give your kids?* It was a tough pill to swallow as I rewatched those moments and realized I am never as compassionate to myself as I am to my children. At the same time, asking that question saved me money in therapy, which felt good. What felt even better was realizing that the fact I asked myself that question means I'm growing. I'm learning. I'm fathering myself first.

The answer to that "why" question is that my inner voice is a bully. It's a concoction made from the bullying I received from my mother and the constant approval I sought from my dad, and I find myself knocking back that toxic cocktail of inner inadequacy whenever I'm struggling with something that feels beyond my abilities.

Unfortunately, as a father, those moments happen frequently. You can smell the feelings of inadequacy on my breath whenever I mutter and grunt my way through difficult tasks. You can hear it in the labels I give myself. You can see the effects of it when I snap in anger because my insecurities are triggered.

My biggest fear is that my inability to hold my proverbial liquor will spill all over my children as they grow older, and they would spend their lives trying to get the smell out of their clothes. I reek of this toxic inner language, and I must stop for the sake of my children and for myself.

Case in point: As I write these words, my truck is stuck in the sand outside our barn. I've tried everything I know to do, but I still can't get it unstuck, so now I have to call a tow truck. The whole time I was working on it, the bully in my head was giving me hell. The voice was my mom's, but the words were my own. *You're inadequate. You procrastinate. You're letting people down. Bruh, you're just lame.* The voice is always like that unless I consciously fight it.

In situations where I lack experience, my inner bully sounds a lot like the character Alonzo from the movie *Training Day*, and my inner child is like Officer Hoyt. If you've seen the film, you might know what I'm talking about. Alonzo is a dirty cop with years of experience and apparent success who tries to intimidate and manipulate his trainee, an idealistic, ambitious young man named Officer Hoyt, by insulting him and lying to him, all in the name of "training." Some of what Alonzo says is true, but most of it is not. And even what *is* half true is infused with toxicity. Hoyt just wants to do what is right and learn how to be a better cop. Alonzo, on the other hand, is mean, manipulative, and abusive—but he does it in such a way that you think maybe he's right and Officer Hoyt needs to listen to him.

Eventually Alonzo's world blows up, and by the end of the movie, his abuse and violence are revealed for what they are: bullying.

I often imagine my inner bully as Alonzo and my inner child as Officer Hoyt. The voice of Alonzo in my head is rude, condescending, aggressive, and flat-out damaging. And yet I listen to it because it claims to be "making me better." So in the name of self-improvement, I abuse myself. I insult myself. I ridicule myself. And then I wonder why it's so hard for me to change.

When you fail, when you don't know something, when you are insecure—what voice do you hear in your head? Whose voice is it, and what does it tell you? Is it building you, or is it bullying you?

An enormous part of fatherhood is instilling the right voice in our children's heads, but we have to do the same for ourselves. When my inner Alonzo tells me I'm green and stupid, I have to father myself. I'll literally say, *Son, if you are lacking experience, you are only one experience away from knowing more than you know now.* I give myself grace to learn and to fail. Well, I try to, anyway. I'm a work in progress, and Alonzo is really convincing.

As I evaluate the mentality I have toward my kids when I'm helping them through a challenging experience, there are three things that I automatically understand about them: *They are dramatic and therefore tend to exaggerate things, they have proof of what they are capable of achieving,* and *they have my force behind them.* If I'm going to father myself, I need to remember that these three things are true about me as well. Let's break them down.

1. THEY ARE DRAMATIC—AND I AM TOO.

The other day Anaya was learning how to skate. We were filming it, of course, and she looked dead into the camera and wailed,

"Daddy, I'm going to die!" Spoiler alert: She didn't die. She was wearing a helmet, we were indoors, and I was holding her by the hand. She was fine. She learned how to skate faster than her brothers did, and now she's a pro.

The girl has always had a flair for the dramatic. I remember when she was four years old, when she was learning to swim. She asked, "What if a shark bites my whole face off, and I get to the hospital and the officers think I'm a bad guy?" This was an indoor pool. No sharks were present, and if any had been, they would've been terrified of *her* because Anaya is a force of nature.

Fear has a language. It has a dialect. Part of fathering is learning to recognize when your kids are being dramatic. This is often called catastrophizing, but I call it being dramatic because they exaggerate everything like bad actors. They don't have a lot of experience yet, and that lack of experience can cause them to imagine dangers that don't exist or reach inaccurate conclusions. Their fear is real, but you as a father know their mindset is not based on reality. You push them to see through their own drama so they can overcome their fear and do what they really want to do.

Here's my point: I am dramatic too. I need to remember this about myself. I get overwhelmed too easily. I see danger bigger than it is. When my insecurities and fear are triggered, I've got to be able to talk myself through that experience. That means being patient with my emotions while *also* not believing all of them. I am not going to die. A shark will not bite my face off. The fear is lying to me, and I'm being dramatic.

To father yourself better, pay attention to your own mental and emotional makeup and learn how to help yourself through your inner drama. In what areas are you dramatic? How does your drama show up? How can you talk yourself out of exaggerated fears? How can you encourage yourself into new things? Are you able to hold yourself accountable when you're making excuses? You know how to do it for your kids. Now do it for yourself too.

2. THEY HAVE PROOF—AND I DO TOO.

Our four kids are proof to each other that they can do hard things, and that helps them overcome challenges and see their own potential. This is especially true for the younger ones because they have the example of their older siblings. For example, it took Theo, our oldest, about forty-five minutes to learn to ride a bike. Considering he has chronic knee issues, that was amazing. He's always been athletic. The process for Uriah was longer—a lot longer. It took me five years to convince him to learn. His exact words on judgment day were, "This is the worst day of my life!" Again, note the drama; apparently it runs in the family.

Anaya watched both processes. She knew it could take her forty-five minutes or five years to learn, but either way, she was going to be riding that bike. Why? Because her brothers were proof. When she got on her bike, Yvette taught her to ride in thirty minutes. Our fourth child, Uzi, learned in about five minutes on Christmas morning.

The principle here is that proof leads to power. We'll unpack this more in a later chapter, but for now, just know that when you can see evidence of what you're capable of achieving, everything changes. Applied to fatherhood, this means that the successes you see in other fathers are proof that you, too, can succeed.

- If other men overcame their past hurts and trauma, so can you.
- If other marriages stood the test of time, so can yours.

- If other fathers built a happy family and peaceful home, so can you.
- If other men are juggling work, home life, marriage, and personal health, so can you.

When my inner bully tells me how bad I am and how hard I'm going to fall, I need to get outside of my own head and look for proof. This idea of proof is the reason I show so much of my family online. As I said earlier, I want to be evidence that fatherhood works, especially for Black fathers who might have grown up without a strong example.

I realized a long time ago that I need a community of people around me, especially other fathers, who can be proof to me that I can get through whatever I happen to be struggling with. Knowing something can be done in theory is one thing, but being in a community of people who do it on the regular creates another level of confidence. I need to be around men who value their fatherhood role and are in a similar season as me. I revel in the moments I have with friends like Kier Gaines and Karega Bailey, among many others, who prove to me that *I am not alone* and *I will be okay*.

WHEN YOU CAN SEE EVIDENCE OF WHAT YOU'RE CAPABLE OF ACHIEVING, EVERYTHING CHANGES.

Who is proof for you? Who shows you what you can aspire to become or do? Who do you call when your strength is gone, or your faith is weak, or you're about to make a wrong decision? Find proof, and you'll find power. You don't have to bootstrap everything. There are people who will pick you up, hold you, inspire you, and challenge you, but only if you let yourself lean on them.

3. THEY HAVE MY FORCE BEHIND THEM—AND I DO TOO.

Whether you are scooting a shopping cart in the parking lot or observing a reaction engine in a rocket, force is force. Having force behind you makes all the difference.

When my kids were learning to ride bikes, they had Yvette and me beside them the whole time, and we wouldn't let them fail. They *fell*, but they didn't *fail*, because we didn't let them. We were a force behind them: guiding them, sustaining them, protecting them, and ultimately launching them into a new level of freedom.

In the same way, I need to remember that I have my own force behind me. That might sound funny, but it's true; I'm not going to let myself fail or quit. I'm not going to give up on myself. I will force myself forward, even if I fall a few times too. Fathering myself means that I provide the inner motivation and force I need to move forward.

As a father, the force you provide for your kids is not the threat of violence but rather the strength to move your kids in the direction they need to go. Sometimes this is against their will, but it's always for their good. I don't know if we have a word in the English language that defines this style of parenting. It's the duality of being both tough and tender. With bike riding, this looks like having one hand on their backs, pushing them forward, and the other on their bike seats, making sure they don't fall. In the pool, this looks like them jumping in while thinking I'm going to catch them, but then sometimes I let them fall through my hands so they can swim back to the top and build their skills and survival instincts.

Let me give you another *Training Day* reference because it's one of my favorite movies. Alonzo was played by Denzel Washington, who won Best Actor at the Academy Awards for this movie and is arguably one of the greatest actors of all time. Denzel is married to Pauletta, and they have a son named John David who is a successful actor in his own right. I've watched interviews with John David, and he doesn't just credit the inspiration he received from his dad. He credits the support he received from his mom. Denzel and John David both sing her praises, and they describe her as creative, thoughtful, loving, and strong. The way I see it, Denzel was proof for John David, but Pauletta was the force behind him. She instilled the guiding principles that carried him toward success.

In my early years as a father, when it was just Theo, Uriah, and me at home, I was less gentle with Theo than I should have been because of my ignorance and inexperience. I led from a lack of sensitivity and a place of frustration. With Uriah, I overcorrected, and I let him choose his own journey too often. I course-corrected yet again, and with Anaya and Uzi, I've learned to be wiser and more hands-on, encouraging them forward through their doubts. Fortunately, Theo and Uriah are still young, and I'm committed to being a tender-and-tough force as I guide them through their childhood.

The crazy thing is that, once again, I often do a poor job of fathering myself this way. I tend to be either too harsh or too hands-off with the child in me. Maybe you've noticed the same tendency in yourself. Often we either beat ourselves up for everything or we let ourselves off the hook for everything. Neither is a great option.

As I write these words, I'm dealing with a lot. Theo has a potential blood clot in his knee, Uriah has an infection that is making his face swell up and break out, it's one hundred degrees outside, and our van is overheating because I hit a coyote on our way to the airport last week. Oh, and my truck is still stuck. In moments like these, I have to *encourage* myself, not bully myself. I need to be my own gentle but unstoppable force.

How about you? You're a force for your kids, but are you a force for you? Do you father yourself in a way that is both gentle *and* powerful, compassionate *and* relentless, understanding *and* demanding?

Trust yourself to be that force. Just like you'd never give up on your kids, you're not going to give up on yourself. Don't listen to the mocking voice inside that says you're going to fail, that you're alone, that your worst fears will come true and somehow you won't be enough. You can be both tough and tender with your inner child, and that force will keep you on course no matter what comes your way.

YOU ARE NOT ALONE

While it's necessary to own your fatherhood role and make sure you are healing, growing, and listening to the right voice inside, please know you are not alone in this process. I've left the most important truth for last: God is your Father. You might not have had the father you needed as a child, but you have the Father you need right now. He's your heavenly Father, and he's with you all the way.

Do you trust him? Do you believe he is with you and is committed to catching you when you fall? That's the hard part, especially when you're staring down the barrel of your own inadequacies. Your heavenly Father has always held you, even when you felt like you were breaking into a million pieces. He's not going to stop now.

I have to father myself into faith all the time, and you probably have as well. I must rely heavily on my understanding of God to keep trusting when my inner child is doubting. I need to be both Pauletta and Denzel, communicating to the little me that I will be okay. Yes, I have responsibilities, pressures, bills, two broken-down cars, two sick kids, and a partridge in a pear tree, but I also have an extremely supportive wife, a community that cares for me, my own hardworking self, and—most important of all—the Creator of the universe.

If you let him, God will not only be your Father; he'll also help you father yourself. He'll let you know when you're being too dramatic. He'll give you proof that you're going to be okay. He'll be the tough and tender force you need to overcome your fears and achieve your goals. He'll help you sort through your bags and figure out whose crap you're carrying and what needs to be thrown away.

Yes, life is crazy at times, and being an adult can feel like a cruel joke. But God's got you, and you've got you, and together, you both have your kids. When you father yourself first, it's a lot easier to be the father your kids need and deserve.

Chapter Number

AN EXPERT ON YOUR CHILDREN

Title

Start

Straight out of high school, I enrolled in college. I'd actually planned to go into the military because I had always despised school, but my mom and my girlfriend's mom sat me down and talked me out of that idea.

In college, money was tight, and I needed a way to make some cash. That's when I met Bo, a fellow student who was about three years older than I was. Bo was a Black Power proponent and a vegan, and he sold oils and incense on campus. He soon became like a big brother to me.

Bo was a fan of the phrase "Each one teach one," which meant that everything he knew, he wanted to pass on to me. That included business skills—the guy was a slick salesman. He taught me chess, and we'd sit in front of the student building playing chess, eating fruit, and burning incense. People who walked by would ask what we were doing, and he'd talk them into buying incense, black soap, or oils.

Along with teaching me about sales, Bo showed me how to cut hair. I quit selling incense after I dropped out of college—which I ended up disliking just as much as high school—but haircutting is something I enjoy to this day. I cut all my kids' hair, and I always have. It's a special time together. I'll forever be grateful to Bo for investing in my life and leaving a deposit that is still giving a return today.

The difference between formal education and the kind Bo gave me is simple: The first was in a classroom, isolated from the real world. That's why I hated it so much. The second was hands-on and practical. Bo didn't just tell me what I needed to know; he showed me. He had me watch him first, then he let me try things for myself.

When it comes to fatherhood, we need to embrace the hands-on learning style that Bo showed me. Reading books about fatherhood is a great start—after all, you're reading one right now—but the best learning happens in the classroom of the home as you interact with your kids. We need to develop our ability to watch them carefully and then put that learning into practice. This isn't a onetime thing either. For the rest of our lives, we'll be studying our kids.

I love how my career choice has given me the opportunity to learn so much about my children because I get to watch and rewatch the videos we make. That's exactly what I do in my "Fatherhood Breakdown" videos: I analyze my kids' thought processes and reactions. Often, when those events were happening in real time, I was predicting what my kids were going to do or say before anything even happened, just because I've spent so much time watching them.

The more I observe my kids and the better I understand what makes them tick, the better father I can be for them.

Everything your kids do and say is a revelation about their inner selves that can help you parent them better. That doesn't mean you have to film them all the time, just that you pay attention to what they do

quote

THE MORE I OBSERVE MY KIDS AND THE BETTER I UNDERSTAND WHAT MAKES THEM TICK, THE BETTER FATHER I CAN BE FOR THEM.

and say, and that you try to understand them better as a result. Those things are breadcrumbs to a lesson, and if you follow them, you might learn something invaluable. They are a thread, and if you pull it, you might get a whole sweater.

Learning is a choice we make every day. As fathers, sometimes we get frustrated by things we should be learning from, and that reaction can sabotage our growth. If we pay attention, we can learn; if we just get aggravated, we probably won't.

Speaking of school, my kids don't exactly hurry through their classwork each day. Sometimes it's because they don't understand the concepts, but usually they're just more interested in hanging out with the family, watching each other work, and watching their parents get slightly frustrated by their slow pace.

That all changed recently when we got them electric dirt bikes. Technically the bikes were Christmas presents, but they opened them two months early because we had to film and edit content for Christmas. That's one of the perks of being the children of an influencer, I guess.

The morning after we gave them the bikes, Uriah woke up super early and came into the kitchen. The first thing he asked was, "Yo, can I ride my dirt bike?"

I told him, "Bro, you haven't even said good morning or brushed your teeth. You're still in your pajamas. You haven't done any schoolwork. No, you can't ride your bike."

I have never seen that kid work so quickly. He's a smart guy, and he got everything done so fast I think he surprised himself. The other kids did the same thing. Now, every day, they whip through their work so they can go ride, because a farm in the middle of the desert is the perfect environment for dirt bikes.

As a dad, I'm paying attention. It's clear that when they dawdle through their work, it's not because they're lazy, the work is too hard, or they're being rebellious; they're just not motivated enough. Rather than being frustrated by that, I need to learn to work with it. I need to keep finding ways to help their motivation levels stay high.

That's what I'm talking about here: paying attention to our children and being open, teachable, and changeable. True fatherhood is about learning, not just teaching. It's about understanding the inner worlds—the motivations, needs, fears, talents, and desires—of our kids rather than simply monitoring their actions so they don't hurt each other or themselves.

That's a lifelong challenge because they keep changing. I feel like I have a master's degree in my wife since we've been married so long, but I'm just now working on college degrees in my kids. I know they'll change once they become teenagers and then adults, so maybe by the time they're in their mid-twenties, I'll have a master's degree in them too. That doesn't mean I'll ever know everything about everyone in my family, but I'll understand them better than I do today and better than I understand anyone else on the planet.

Let me give you three phrases that sum up the kind of learning we need to engage in as fathers. First, learn *about* your kids; second, learn *from* your kids; and third, learn *for* your kids. Let's look at each of these.

LEARN ABOUT YOUR KIDS

I started my YouTube channel when Theo and Uriah were toddlers. A lot of what they would say was unintelligible to anyone outside our family, so I'd spend hours each week poring over the audio files and captioning the videos. I got to the point where I could look at the waveform of an audio file and know which kid was speaking just by their cadence, inflection, and volume.

Since those early videos the kids' pronunciation has improved, and so has YouTube's auto-captioning feature, so I don't have to analyze their speech anymore. Their individual response patterns stuck with me though, and even today, when I ask them questions, you can catch me anticipating their words and almost mouthing their responses.

The idea that each child has a unique cadence fascinates me. Just as their speech has a specific cadence, so do their thoughts, their actions, and their decisions. That means I need to become an expert in parenting my children as distinct individuals. Before I had kids, I would have assumed having four children would be like having four slightly tweaked versions of the same kid. After all, they have the same dad and the same mom. In reality, of course, they are four entirely different people, which means I have to pay attention to each one, study each one, and learn each one.

With Theo, our oldest, one experience will forever stick in my mind as a father. When he was a small child, he had locs. That was partly for safety because if he ever got lost, he'd be a lot easier to describe with a unique hairstyle; and it was partly because he looked really cute with locs. Over the years, I spent a lot of time with him twisting his locs. He wasn't really a cuddler, but when I was twisting his hair, he'd sit on my lap for two hours straight. Those were bonding times for us.

I didn't realize how important Theo's locs were to me until he told me, "Dad, I want to cut my hair" when he was six years old. It's hard to describe what I felt. It was grief, I suppose, because I knew I was saying goodbye to the little child I had known. I've always been my boys' barber. So when it was clear that Theo wanted this, I got out my scissors and clippers, and I cut his locs off and gave him an even Caesar with a shape-up.

It changed his entire appearance. We could see his forehead, his eyes, and his ears. We even found out he had a birthmark on the back of his head that none of us knew about. He instantly looked three years older.

More than his appearance, though, his personality blossomed. He smiled bigger and acted with more confidence. He took up hockey soon after that, a sport that is now a huge part of his life. I look back on that haircut as a defining moment in his development from a child into a preteen. It was emotional for me, but it was liberating for him.

What I learned was that I had to let him tell me about himself. I couldn't hold him captive to the person he'd been in the past. I had to step back and allow him to discover and reveal himself, and I had to accept and embrace the new, growing version of the child I'd always known.

That was not the last time I'll do that with Theo or with any of my kids. They're growing and flourishing in front of my eyes. My challenge now—and for the rest of my life—is to learn about who they are becoming each day, even if it means saying goodbye to something I loved from the past.

Uriah, our second, is very different from his brother. He and I have spent a lot of time together because I became a stay-at-home dad soon after he was born, so I've watched him grow and develop. He is always affectionate, always passionate, and always *loud*. I wish the kid had volume control.

One thing I've learned about Uriah is that if I push him too hard, he'll get overwhelmed and start to panic. Then, if I react to his emotions and yell at him, he'll shut down. Now, in some ways, parenting is like coaching, and I know coaches often yell at their players. On the sports field, that might be an effective way to communicate, but coaches don't tuck their players in at night. They're coaches, and that's it. As fathers, we have many hats to wear and many roles to fill. We're teachers, chefs, problem-solvers, moderators, and more. So we have to make sure we don't show up in a way that causes us to lose access in other ways.

Something we recently learned about Uriah is that he has ADHD along with high-functioning autism. Those things don't define him, but they are part of who he is and how he interacts with the world. My wife had been telling me for some time that in the classroom, he was different from the other kids. For example, he had fidgeting episodes and would start crying if more than one sound was occurring at a time. I just thought Yvette didn't know how to handle the situation. Not until I started helping homeschool the kids did I see it too, and I realized how much I didn't know.

Learning this about Uriah is causing me to rethink a lot of things I assumed, both about him and about fatherhood—and that's my point here. This "learn about your kids" process is a normal, healthy part of being a parent. Each new kid and each new stage of growth will require you to reconsider what you think you know, adjust your expectations and assumptions, and move forward with more accurate knowledge.

Our third child and only daughter is Anaya. Even though she's only seven, she has me figured out more than the other three put together. She is "high saddity," which is Black vernacular for someone with expensive taste and high expectations. For example, when she was three, she loved a snack called Veggie Sticks. These little snacks came in three colors: green, yellow, and orange. Although there was no difference in flavor between those three colors, Anaya refused to eat any color except orange. If we gave her a full bowl, she'd leave two-thirds untouched. Rather than fighting that battle over and over, Yvette would separate the orange ones every time she opened a bag and save them for Anaya. It was insane.

More recently, when I was going to be gone for three days to work on this book, Anaya made a list of all the things she wanted to do while I was away. I said, "Okay, show me the list." She was like, "Eat at In-N-Out, have a marshmallow challenge, ride an elephant . . ." That was her expectation for the next three days.

I said, "You're so high-maintenance. Where'd you get that from?"

Immediately she pointed at her mom, who was swinging in a $600 hammock I'd bought her for her birthday, and said, "From her."

With Anaya, I am scared of what's coming because she thinks the rules don't apply to her, and somehow she finds ways to get me to do what she wants. It's bizarre. I love her, but she terrifies me sometimes. I'm still trying to figure her out, but it seems like she's already got *me* figured out and is always one step ahead. Something tells me I'm always going to be playing catch-up with this one. Again, that's the point: You will always be learning about your kids. Don't let that frustrate you. Let it intrigue you. Let it fascinate you.

Our youngest is Uziah. As I write these words, he's only five, so describing him is hard because he's still coming into his personality. I can say that when he was two, he'd get mad and just haul off and hit people on the regular. We have it documented on video. Now, he's calmed down—a little. He beats up on his siblings maybe once a week rather than every hour. I guess you'd call that progress. He's in the testing-the-limits stage, trying to figure out what he can get away with. He's a blend of the other three kids because he's around them all the time, but I have no doubt in my mind that he's going to develop in specific directions as he grows older. I can't wait to see what directions those are.

Kids are like surprise packages. You don't know what's hidden inside. The difference is, you don't open them; they have to open themselves. You just keep them alive while that process happens.

I've come to realize with all my kids that what I find irritating about them is often connected to their specific gifts. Whether their questions, their strength, their emotional outbursts, their drama, or their nonstop chatter, what I'm looking at is the seeds of their future strengths. Right now, they're practicing. They don't always know how to handle those abilities or play to those strengths. That's where I come in. It's my job to see those things, hone them, and invest in them.

LEARN FROM YOUR KIDS

Kids are smarter than we usually give them credit for, and if we pay attention, they'll often tell us what we need to know about them and what they need from us. As they teach us more about themselves, we will become better parents.

One time Theo was trying to outdo his brother on his bike, and he fell really hard. He actually fractured both of his wrists, although we didn't know it at the time. He was clearly in pain, but when he carried on and seemed to be doing okay, we thought he just needed some time. More than anything, I was irritated that he was trying to show off. Not until a week later, when he fell again and started yelling in pain, did we realize how bad he had been injured from the first fall.

I felt terrible. I wished I would have paid more attention. Theo has always had a high pain tolerance, though, and he never wants to be a burden. He often won't tell us what he's feeling or how he's hurting. I've learned that with him. I have to ask a lot of questions and pay attention to the nuances of his answers. If I listen, he'll give me clues to what he needs, and he'll invite me closer.

I don't mean just physically but also mentally and emotionally. For example, because of the fall, he got a cast on one arm and a brace on the other. One day, we were joking around, and he said something halfway aggressive to me. I popped off with "What are you gonna do? Beat me with your cast?" It was all in good fun in my mind, and I had like twenty more broken-arm jokes in the queue. But he got upset. He got a little moody, and he told me I hurt his feelings.

Part of me was bothered by that, and I thought, *Wow, I can't seem to do anything right*. But I realized he was trying to tell me that he's not as emotionally strong as he pretends to be. He always acts like things don't bother him, but they do. His honesty with me was an invitation to listen and learn. I had to accept the invitation. My twenty jokes were funny, but they would not have gone over well. I had to be sensitive to his needs in that moment.

If you listen with a humble, patient heart, you can usually figure out what your child needs. That understanding is gold; it enables you to be the father *they* need in *that* specific context. That might not look like what your dad gave you or what you imagined yourself doing for your kids, but that's not what matters. What matters is their well-being, and as their father, you are God's provision for their needs. Maybe it's a hug. Maybe it's crying together. Maybe it's tickling them or chasing them around the house. Maybe it's a spontaneous trip. Maybe it's inviting them to help you with a project. What they need seems like an enigma sometimes, but you're the best person to make sense of it.

Besides revealing what they need, they'll also show you how you need to change—if you're willing to learn. This will stretch you because you'll have to do things outside your comfort zone. I'm not saying you need to be someone you were not created to be, but you will need to become *all* you were created to be. None of us have it all together when we first become parents. We learn and grow along the way, and our best teachers are the kids we're loving and caring for.

Recently my daughter was whispering to my wife, and I could hear her say, "Hey, I want to tell dad . . ." Then she said something I couldn't hear. My wife said, "Well, just tell him." It took Anaya a minute to get up the nerve to say, "Dad, I want to use the white fan."

So backstory: She was talking about the fan I bought for my office, which was *my* fan. It's mad hot in our house in the summer, and we have several fans, but Anaya kept sticking her fingers in the blades and breaking them. (The blades, not her fingers.) Besides that, all the kids would stand on the bases of the fans and push them, which would break them too. This had happened multiple times, and I had

quote

I'M NOT SAYING YOU NEED TO BE SOMEONE YOU WERE NOT CREATED TO BE, BUT YOU WILL NEED TO BECOME *ALL* YOU WERE CREATED TO BE.

made my frustration clear. I knew I should install a ceiling fan, but do-it-yourself stuff isn't really my thing.

Her hesitancy to talk to me was a wake-up call. It told me I was being too intense and grumpy about the whole thing. If my daughter can't even approach me about something as basic as a fan, what does that reveal about how she sees me and how I present myself? On an inner level, I was reminded to quit overreacting to things just because they highlight my deficiency as a handyman. I didn't say any of that out loud. I just told her that of course she could borrow the fan—but not to break it. Then I made a mental note to calm down a little about the whole fan situation. Her reaction showed me how I needed to change so I could parent her better, but I had to pay attention and learn the lesson.

LEARN FOR YOUR KIDS

The goal of learning is to become a better parent for your kids. Ultimately, their well-being matters most. We want to meet them where they are, then father them forward.

When I was a kid, I don't think my dad knew how to show me affection. I'd see him only in the summer, and it seemed like he was just waiting for me to get older so we could play sports together and joke around. Now, as a grown-up, I love the bantering between us. But I needed something different when I was eleven years old. I needed affection.

With my kids, if Uriah needs a hug, he's getting a hug. I might tell him to go get a shower because he's in that funky stage of human development, but I'll hug him first. I've learned that I need to meet him where he is at, not expect him to meet me where I'm at. That's why learning about each child is so important. The lessons enable you to parent with understanding and empathy.

Too often, I think we try to parent our kids toward our preference for them. We want to control the outcome a little too much. While we can be a strong influence for them, we should also keep in mind that we exist for them, not the other way around. They didn't ask to be born. We chose that for them. Now it's up to us to guide and empower them to become the people God meant for them to be.

There's a story in the Bible about how John the Baptist told his followers he needed to decrease so that Jesus could increase. John recognized his role was to become less visible over time as Jesus stepped into his calling and became more visible. That's a good way to describe the transition that happens with parents and children.

At first, you're the hero, the king, and the boss (as well as the servant, the cook, and the butt-wiper). Eventually, your kids grow up and take more responsibility for themselves. If you're lucky, they even take showers without being told to. (So far only one of my kids has achieved that level of independence.) Along the way, you fade into the background a little more with each stage. You're still there, but you intentionally make their growth about them, not about you. You decrease so they can increase.

When parents refuse to do this, they often veer into codependence, which is about needing to feel needed. Codependent parents keep their kids dependent on them for too long or in unhealthy ways. That's dysfunctional though. Codependence is not good for the parents or the children. It's far better to figure out what our kids need in each stage, provide it for them, and consistently push them toward greater independence and maturity.

Remember, you have only a few years with them when they're young and moldable, then you'll have a few more when they're teenagers and need you in different ways. After that, although they'll still need you, your influence will be from a distance. So take full advantage of the time you have with them now. Study them. Learn about them and learn from them. Learn about yourself too.

Then take all that learning and use it to serve your children. If you become an expert in your kids, your fatherhood will reach a whole new level.

02

Part Number

EXPECTATIONS

Title

Start

Nothing and nobody can fully prepare you for fatherhood. Kids do, say, wear, and eat the craziest things. That's why when parents get together, we usually trade horror stories and laugh so we don't cry.

Expectations are powerful, and they can work for us or against us. On one hand, if we have healthy expectations, we'll be able to navigate the ups and downs of parenthood without getting too shocked by what happens along the way. That's why it's helpful to have access to other people's lives so we can see the power of fatherhood and learn what it looks like in real life. This is the topic of **chapter 3, "Proof Is Power."**

On the other hand, if we have overly idealistic expectations of what parenting looks like, we won't be prepared for the chaos and craziness that children are naturally gifted at creating. In **chapter 4, "They'll Throw Up in Your Mouth,"** we talk about expecting the unexpected and becoming more resilient and adaptable, even when life is chaotic and plans don't work out.

03

Chapter Number

PROOF IS POWER

Title

Start

A little over decade ago, my wife of five years asked me a question that changed my life. We had tucked in the boys and were in bed, but Yvette couldn't sleep. She stared at me and said, "I'm bored. Tell me a bedtime story so I can fall asleep."

I, being a creative person, understood the mental energy that would take and was irritated by the request. I jokingly responded, "What do I look like, Dr. Seuss? I'm tired too!"

We both laughed, and once the room fell silent, she smiled and said, "Well, tell me your five-year plan."

That was a totally unfair request because it was eleven o'clock at night and I was half asleep, so all I could think to say was, "Well, you know . . . whatever God has for us. I'm just trusting him."

She replied, "Hmm . . . I'm trusting you with my family and my future, and you don't even have five years planned out?" Then she rolled over and went to sleep.

I don't think she'll ever understand how much that question hurt. It exposed so much of me as a husband and a father: my lack of vision, my lack of direction. It challenged my manhood. To be fair, she did throw me a softball first with the bedtime story request. I should have just made up a story. Instead, I found myself staring at the ceiling, questioning my entire existence.

At the time, I had just turned thirty years old. We had two children. I was traveling off and on and making music, and Yvette was working as a math teacher. Over the next few days, I got really frustrated with myself, and I knew I needed a plan. So I went to talk to a good friend of mine named Scotty James, who is very practical and asks good questions. My wife is insightful, but sometimes she'll just say things and walk away, and I'll be left standing there like the end piece on a loaf of bread. I needed something more concrete.

"Don't just think five years ahead," Scotty told me. "Where do you see yourself in fifteen years?"

"I don't know," I said, "but when I'm forty-five, I know I don't want to be on a stage talking about, 'put your hands up.'"

"What do you want to be doing?"

"I want to be writing music for other people, and I want to be telling people how great it is to be a father, because I never knew how good it could be."

"Whoa, wait," he said. "Really?"

"Yeah."

"Well, you're already writing music. Tell me more about this fatherhood stuff. Who do you want to be speaking to? Where are they now? Where will they be in fifteen years? How can you reach them?"

By the time I left his office, I had a blueprint for a social presence that I knew would impact future families—especially fathers—over the next fifteen years.

At this point, I had been a stay-at-home dad for about nine months. The backstory there is that Yvette had come up with a crazy idea: Because all the money I was making at my warehouse job was going to childcare, she suggested I stay home. I could make extra money by moonlighting as a rapper. She thought it made more sense for me to take care of the two boys because her job provided health insurance and other benefits, and mine did not. She also told me it would be cool for them to see their dad modeling love for them since they are both boys.

I was reluctant at first. More accurately, I hated the idea, mostly because I thought my friends and family would judge me for not working. I had no idea how much work it took to raise an infant and chase a toddler on the daily. And so, ignorant of my pending workload and with a zeal for hip-hop, I began my stay-at-home dad journey. Soon *Sesame Street* was playing for the kids during waking hours, while nap time and bedtime were dedicated to my rap career with my crew, the Dream Junkies.

Nothing could have prepared me for the emotional and physical fatigue that comes with 24-7 parenting. Along with that there is a desperation and a feeling of not being seen that I couldn't have imagined. I now understand how women feel when their husband gets home and complains that the dishes aren't done. My wife would walk into the house, survey the scene, and give me a look that said, "What did you do today?"

"Nobody died today. That's what I did. They're alive and the house is not on fire."

I quickly learned that parenting a newborn and a two-year-old sucked, but I also felt a sense of fulfillment I have never experienced before. It was exhausting but also purpose-filled, intimate, and vulnerable. All these things were true, and no one had ever told me—like a secret that should've been exposed. Fatherhood is life-altering, and I am living proof.

After talking with Scotty, my fifteen-year plan came to life. I decided I would close my chapter as a touring rapper and begin to tell people the truth about fatherhood, because the biggest stage I'd ever stand on would be my living room. On October 19, 2015, I uploaded the first episode of *Beleaf in Fatherhood*.

My videos started as a way to document the trials and tribulations of fatherhood along with the victories. I figured people wouldn't believe what I was experiencing unless I showed them. Not just the six poopy diapers a day but the good parts too. The joy of watching your kid learn something new, the peace on their faces when they fall asleep in your arms, the way they laugh when you're tickling them—until they punch you in the balls and the game is over.

As I said earlier, proof is power, and I need to experience things in order to learn them. I need to see them in action, not just hear about them. And judging by the comments and DMs I get on the regular, most of us are that way. We need to see what is possible. We need proof.

My family is not the only healthy family out there, of course. All around us are countless healthy, successful families, but we have to notice them, and we have to believe their story can be ours too. If we look for proof that our families will fail, we'll find it. And if we look for proof that we'll succeed, we'll find it. The question is, Are we looking at the right proof?

Remember, too, that "proof" is not the same thing as "rules." I can barely figure out how to be a relatively good father to my kids. I still spend most of my day keeping them alive and trying not to burn down the house. The point isn't to do fatherhood how somebody else does it but to figure out what *your* kids need and do that.

If we can all be proof of how good family can be, just imagine how soon we could rewrite the narrative society has about fatherhood, as well as the narratives in our heads. In one generation, we could change everything. We could raise kids who aren't carrying bags from the past and who fully believe in themselves and in their capability as parents. That's a dream worth pursuing.

ACCESS IS EVERYTHING

To see proof of fatherhood and family, you need access to places and people who will raise the bar for you. It's one thing to stand outside and try to figure out what makes a family successful and happy, but it's another to be invited into someone's home.

This is the primary motivation behind the fatherhood videos I make. I want to create a space where people can experience the highs and lows of family, especially if their upbringing didn't necessarily set them up for success, which was the case for me.

IF WE CAN ALL BE PROOF OF HOW GOOD FAMILY CAN BE, JUST IMAGINE HOW SOON WE COULD REWRITE THE NARRATIVE SOCIETY HAS ABOUT FATHERHOOD.

quote

I don't usually clean up my house or fix up my kids before I shoot a video. There are toys everywhere. Everybody's got ashy knees and messy hair, and usually at least one child isn't wearing a shirt. Sometimes dishes are piled in the sink, or a dog is running around with a cone on her head in the background, or there is mysterious, unclaimed poop on the ground. I even have to bleep out an occasional curse word (from my mouth, not the kids'), especially when reptiles have gotten loose in our house.

Why? Because that's what real life looks like—and that's exactly the point. Why would I fake anything? Portraying a lie doesn't help anyone. I'd rather give people access to my family, vulnerable as that feels, in the hope of inspiring others. The reason I feel so strongly about this is because my life was changed by the access other people gave me to their families.

Mr. Hale is the first person who comes to mind. He was the father of my friend Sydney, and he lived with his family on the bottom floor of our apartment building. I lived on the top floor with my mom and little brother. When I was about ten years old, I would often walk down four flights of stairs and knock on the door of their cramped apartment.

Stepping into their living room was like entering another universe. One of my core memories is seeing my friend and his two brothers jumping off the couch and slamming into their dad while he chased them around the room making sound effects and pretending to be a superhero. He would be wearing nothing but a cape and what we called dun-ta-duns (aka tighty-whities). The dude had no shame. He just loved playing with his kids. While I remember feeling slightly disturbed to discover that you'll have hair on your thighs when you're a grown man, watching Mr. Hale take so much delight in goofing off with his family was inspiring. I didn't experience that kind of play with my father because he lived on the other side of the country, and when I visited, he didn't seem like he knew what someone my age wanted to do. Mr. Hale's dun-ta-duns superhero games were the basis for what my kids and I call Blanket Warrior, which is when I put a blanket over my head and they take turns attacking me. It's one of their favorite things to do with me, and I owe it to a man who was willing to let me come into his home and just watch his family and his parenting.

Another person who gave me access was Dr. Carson, who is the grandfather of my brother, Blease. From the time Dr. Carson entered my life, he treated me as a grandchild. He didn't have to do that because we weren't related by blood, and my mom and his son were never married, but Dr. Carson and his wife—who I also called Dr. Carson, because she was a doctor too—accepted me into their home and family anyway. He took me under his wing. He taught me to play golf. He showed genuine interest in me, and along the way he modeled what it meant to be a father.

He's eighty-five now, but we stay in touch. We've visited the Carsons on family road trips, and I still talk on the phone with him. Recently I called him up and asked him why he gave me so much access, and he told me that to him, I was always family. He said he liked me, and he didn't like most teenagers. Then he told me how proud he is of who I've become and how I care so much for my family, and he said he loves me. I broke down in tears on the phone. That was the first time I'd heard him say he loved me, although there was never any doubt in my mind that he does. The impact he and his wife have had on me—and by extension, my family—is immeasurable.

Finally, and maybe most importantly from a fatherhood perspective, is Pat, one of the pastors at my church. I mentioned him earlier. Pat gave me access to his home and became a mentor to me in my early twenties. Pat and his wife have seven daughters, and I remember walking into his house and being overwhelmed by peace. It was loud and there were people everywhere, but nobody was screaming or bullying anyone. Things just seemed to function. The oldest was doing the dishes. The second oldest was holding the baby. Two other sisters were playing together. And they were all so welcoming to me.

That was totally different from my upbringing. When I was growing up in my mom's house, if people came over, I know they could tell tensions were high. Pat's home was proof that family could work. I was amazed by the peace, by the way they got along, and by how welcoming it felt. I wanted to stay there, not leave. I suddenly saw what family could look like, and for the first time ever, I could envision myself in the role of a father.

At crucial moments in my life, these three men gave me access to a world I wasn't familiar with, and as a result, I grew and changed. I don't necessarily parent the same way they did, but I am indebted to them for letting me learn from them.

Who are your Mr. Hales, your Dr. Carsons, your Pats? Who do you *have* access to, and who are you *giving* access to? Those two questions should follow all of us throughout our lives. Even now, I learn from other people. I have a community of like-minded fathers, and we inspire and educate each other. I'm convinced that if we're going to be good fathers, we need to *see* proof for ourselves, and we need to *be* proof for others.

This is harder than you might think. A big problem for men is that society normalizes the challenges of motherhood and celebrates mothers who are actively involved in raising their kids, but fathers get treated differently. I remember as a stay-at-home dad, I'd take my kids to the park. I noticed the moms who were there with their kids would connect easily with each other, but nobody was coming over to talk to me because I was a guy. Moms get together and have brunches and share about their challenges and techniques, but when was the last time you sat with a group of dads and talked about those things?

Our role, according to stereotypes, is to provide, protect, and discipline; but we're not really given permission to feel anything, to struggle with anything, or to admit we need help with the day-to-day challenges of diapers, homework, and a million other parenting realities. Because of that, we can feel alone and isolated, with no one to talk to, dump on, or learn from.

As I mentioned before, the realization that men often feel alone in their fatherhood experience was what drove me to invest so much time in creating videos. When I became a stay-at-home dad, I was in an unfamiliar world, a world where I often felt alone, overwhelmed, and unseen. I knew if I was feeling those things, other men were too. But it was also a world of incredible joy, where I got to experience moments with my young kids that many dads don't get to see, and I wanted to share that as well.

For all of us fathers, giving and receiving access requires intentionality and commitment. Society isn't going to fix its limited, toxic view of fatherhood by itself. We need to change what is "normal" in our role. That starts by connecting with other dads and seeing other proof. It starts with gaining access and giving access. To my kids, Blanket Warrior is just as important as bringing home a paycheck, but I wouldn't have known that without Mr. Hale. Unconditional acceptance and love are basic elements of a solid family, but I needed Dr. Carson to model that for me. Peace and harmony are possible in a home, but I had to see it in Pat's life before I could believe it was possible for mine.

Maybe you can't look back on your formative years and find many positive examples of fatherhood, but who can you look to today? Who can you learn from now? I'd encourage you to intentionally gain more access by connecting with other dads. If there's someone near you who has a family you admire, ask him what he did to get what he has. Read books about fatherhood, watch videos about fatherhood, ask questions about fatherhood. The more access you give yourself to positive examples, the more accurate your expectations will be.

THE POWER IN PROOF

Proof is power, and access is what provides proof. Let me break this down more specifically by giving you three things proof does for us as fathers.

1. PROOF REMINDS US HOW MUCH INFLUENCE WE HAVE.

The movie *King Richard*, which is about how tennis superstars Serena and Venus Williams began their careers, is so inspiring to me. It portrays a man who is committed to his daughters' success and who helps change the course of their lives. I've also read about Earl Woods, who is Tiger Woods's father, and about Joe Jackson, Michael Jackson's father. While I don't necessarily share all of their parenting philosophies, the sheer force of fatherhood is evident in how they helped influence and motivate their kids.

> **PROOF IS POWER, AND ACCESS IS WHAT PROVIDES PROOF.**
>
> *quote*

We often forget how powerful fatherhood is. Think about this though: The lack of fathers in the home is often cited as a reason why kids struggle or why generational cycles of poverty and addiction continue. If that's right, then the opposite must also be true: Our presence makes a real, tangible, powerful difference. We need to believe that truth and see ourselves as catalysts for our kids' success.

That's the power of seeing the influence other fathers have with their children: It raises the bar for us. It reminds us that we are making a difference, one unclogged toilet at a time. Life has a way of beating up on us and telling us that our efforts are too little, that we're not enough, that our mistakes have more power than our successes, but it's not true. Set your focus on proof of positive fatherhood and let yourself be inspired by what your presence can and will accomplish.

2. PROOF SETS REALISTIC EXPECTATIONS.

When I found out I was going to be a dad, I went to eight or nine seasoned men who were fathers and asked them to tell me the top three things they wanted their kids to learn before they grew up and left the house. They spoke about integrity, money management, self-control, self-confidence, and work ethic. Not a single person said he was teaching his kids to fight. That shocked me, because I grew up in Baltimore. I just assumed that a good dad would make sure his kids knew how to throw down. The things the men said were so sentimental and internal, and it bugged me at the time. Now that I have four kids of my own, I completely agree. I had to change my expectations.

None of us is born knowing how to be a father; it's a learned skill. That's why it's so important to have access to other father figures so we can get a clearer picture of what this job actually entails. Expectations that are not aligned with reality are a setup for discouragement and bad decisions.

When you see other families in action, you rethink what you thought you knew. That usually means lowering your expectations in some areas and showing yourself self-compassion, and it means raising those expectations in other areas and demanding more of yourself. Either way, the better you can align your expectations with reality, the more you'll enjoy the fatherhood journey.

3. PROOF SHOWS US WHAT IS POSSIBLE.

Anaya was born at home, which was something Pat's family inspired us to do. I can honestly say I've never felt as much peace as I did on the day she came into this world. In the hospital, all you hear between contractions are lights buzzing, machines beeping, and hospital noise. At home, we heard birds chirping. They would stop singing whenever Yvette started a contraction, as if they knew what was happening. Theo and Uriah were with us. There came a point at which Theo left the room because he didn't like hearing his mom cry out, which is totally fine. I respect his awareness of his own limits. Uriah really stepped up though. He held her hand, patted her back, and told her, "It's okay. You're going to be okay, Mommy."

I can't even put into words the beauty of that whole experience. I felt peace. I felt family unity. I felt gratitude. I watched the family operate as a unit, and we were stronger together. In that moment, I heard the Holy Spirit tell me, *It can be this way all the time.* I think about that phrase a lot. God was raising my expectations for my family, and he was showing me a possible future. I could have a family that truly flourished, that loved and cared for each other, and that radiated peace. Once I caught a glimpse of what was possible, I could believe in it and work toward it.

In the same way, when we see tangible proof of what families can become, we are given something to believe and work for. The success, joy, and peace that others achieve are indications of what is possible for us, just as our families are inspirations for others as well.

I'll say it again: We need to *gain* access, and we need to *give* access to others. That's how we'll change our world, but even more importantly, it's how we'll become the fathers we need to be.

Whether you've got a five-year plan, fifteen-year plan, or fifty-year plan, I hope it includes family. Yes, you should have an idea where your career is going. Yes, you should think about investments and retirement. Yes, you should pray about what ministries you're going to be a part of. But while you're doing all that, catch a vision for what your fatherhood is doing for your children. They're blessed to have you as their dad, and your investment in them is making a difference. Your efforts will prove to *them* that fatherhood matters.

04

Chapter Number

THEY'LL THROW UP IN YOUR MOUTH

Title

Start

When I found out I was going to be a father, I started asking some of my friends who were fathers about what was coming. I expected practical advice from the trenches, but instead they mostly just tried to scare me.

They'd shake their heads and mutter, "Man, everything's about to change. You'll never sleep again. You'll never have time alone with your wife. You'll never go out with your friends. You'll never have enough money." They took great delight in telling me horror stories from their own parenting. It was haunting, like *Tales from the Crypt*.

But nobody ever said, "Glen, they're gonna throw up in your mouth, so here's what you do . . ." That would have been helpful information. Nobody told me that when that happens—because it will—make sure you don't swallow. Set the kid down immediately, bend over, clear the roof of your mouth first, then spit it out. I had to learn that myself, the hard way.

Honestly, I don't blame them for not being more specific. There are so many things that happen to you as a father that being fully prepared is impossible. You can (and should) learn everything possible before you have kids, but to be the father you need to be, you have to expect the unexpected.

EXPECT THE UNEXPECTED

While you can't figure everything out beforehand, you can get better at figuring things out as you go. If you're too locked into your own expectations, you'll only make it harder for yourself and your kids because kids do crazy things—unhinged, illogical, astonishing things that make you question how humanity has survived this long.

I have stories for days. One time I was on the toilet and Uriah had to go to the bathroom. He was maybe two years old. He couldn't wait, so he found a shaving cream cap and just started peeing in it. The cap was way too small, but even worse, it had a hole in the bottom. So I'm sitting there yelling at him while I'm trying to finish up, helplessly watching pee streaming out of the hole in the cap.

On another occasion, Theo—also around two years old—wiped his butt and then his face with the same tissue. I couldn't believe it. What was the kid thinking? Was he even thinking at all?

I remember when we moved out of our first place, we found a banana that had been left on a dresser at some point long ago. It had decayed over time and melted into the dresser. Why was a banana there, and how did it possibly sit there so long it literally became part of the wood, like some fossil record revealing that the Henry kids had once lived there?

Even after four kids, I'm still unprepared. When Uzi was two, he realized everyone had a name, including his parents, and it fascinated him. Every night for weeks, I would put them all to bed, and later, Uzi would creep downstairs and sit on the stairs by the kitchen in total darkness. Suddenly I'd hear a faint, creepy voice asking,

"What's your name?" I'd turn around, and the baby would be there. It was utterly terrifying.

Being a father is trying to figure out why your kids' hands are blue. What is blue in our house? Where did this blue substance even come from? It's trying to understand how they have toothpaste lodged in their hair. Like, what part of the evening routine could've possibly resulted in toothpaste getting all the way up there? It's trying to know how to react when they say their first curse word. Do you laugh or scold them?

To be honest, I thought fatherhood would be less messy. You'd think by now I would have learned my lesson, but I still find myself expecting that somehow, against all odds, today will be less messy. Today will go according to plan. Today is the day my kids will miraculously behave like the adults they will some-day be.

In those moments, I have to remind myself that my unrealistic expectations are not doing me any favors. Sometimes my kids don't have to change; my expectations do.

- Nothing will go according to plan.
- Everything will take longer than I think.
- I don't know what's coming.
- I don't know what I will need.
- I don't know how I'm going to deal with it.
- I don't know how to prepare.
- Somebody will probably throw up in my mouth.

That is all normal. It's okay. And it's *within our capabilities* as fathers. The sooner we make peace with the chaos and randomness of trying to raise tiny humans-in-training, the sooner we'll enjoy parenting rather than let it get under our skin.

THE MESS IS NECESSARY

I've come to understand that not only is the chaos inevitable; it's necessary. The unexpectedness of fatherhood is a vital part of the path forward.

People want parenting to be like math: rational, predictable, and repeatable. It's actually more like science though. Do you remember the scientific method? You create a hypothesis, you test it out, and then you refine it and keep going. Parenting is essentially a long series of trial-and-error experiments. That's what I mean when I say the mess is necessary; it's moving you forward. The experiments constantly reveal more about your kids, more about you, and more about what you can become together.

SOMETIMES MY KIDS DON'T HAVE TO CHANGE; MY EXPECTATIONS DO.

quote

When I was asking my friends what to expect, I was looking for math answers. I thought I could reduce parenting to a set of rules. I assumed, for example, that if I prioritized bedtime and let kids cry it out, then they would become independent and self-sufficient. Logically, that would mean less work for me.

That's the wrong way to approach fatherhood though. I can't parent for my own convenience. If my goal is to teach my kids that they should solve all their own problems and be fully independent, I'm actually teaching them how *not* to be part of a family system. They won't know how to ask for help, accept help, or give help.

Beware of wanting to reduce fatherhood to rules that make life easier for us as parents. Often what's good for *our* present isn't best for *their* future. That's not a legacy move; it's a convenience one. Remember, we're not just parenting children; we're raising adults. If our goal each day is just to get them to behave and not cause us too much grief, we're overlooking the future.

This is why I stopped spanking our kids a long time ago. I remember the day it happened. Theo was about four years old, and every time I went to work, he would growl and bark at his mom like a dog. We couldn't get him to stop. I was going to spank him, but Yvette stopped me. She said, "You're teaching him to fear you but not to communicate." So instead of a quick spanking, I spent two hours trying to help him understand why he couldn't bark at his mom. I had a whiteboard and everything. It wasn't a convenient way to handle the situation, but it was a much better one.

In the Bible, Paul wrote, "For our light and momentary troubles are achieving for us an eternal glory that far outweighs them all. So we fix our eyes not on what is seen, but on what is unseen, since what is seen is temporary, but what is unseen is eternal" (2 Corinthians 4:17–18). Paul didn't have kids, so he wasn't talking about fatherhood—but he could have been. The principle is the same. The bad stuff and inconveniences don't feel "light and momentary" when they are happening, but they are achieving something monumental and long-lasting. They are creating a future that is unseen right now but will be wonderful when we finally experience it.

The unexpectedness and messiness of parenting is something to embrace because it means your children are growing, learning, and becoming who they're meant to be. You get a front-row seat to the process. It's a movie you've never seen, a song you've never listened to, a destination you've not yet reached. That is exciting! I promise you, there is wonder along the way. Also barf. But mostly wonder.

PREPARING FOR WHAT YOU CAN'T PREDICT

While you can't always know what to expect, you can still prepare. Your preparation will just look different from what you might have assumed it would before having kids. Here are a few suggestions.

1. BUILD IN MARGIN FOR ERROR.

It's funny how often I expect the impossible and then get frustrated when it doesn't happen. I don't know why I do this. My kids act like kids, and somehow it surprises me. I have to remind myself regularly that too-high expectations are setups for aggravation. That's on me, not my kids.

While you might have been able to execute your plans perfectly when you were single or married without kids, it's just not going to happen now. Don't merely accept that fact; plan for it. Build in some margin. Leave room for error. Bring three extra onesies, not just one. Pack an extra shirt for yourself too. Have backup wipes in the car. Leave a little early. You can't predict the delays or distractions, but you can build in enough margin to handle them gracefully.

Things like time and extra clothes are obvious areas that need margin, but another area is even more important: your mental and emotional state. Too often we live teetering on the edge of stressed-out, and then a kid drops a vase, shaves the dog, or writes on the table with Sharpie, and we lose our minds. I've been there more times than I care to recall. We all know that in those moments, the issue we're mad about isn't the real issue—but it's the straw that broke Dad Camel's back. The real issue is that we're too tense, tired, or worried to handle the normal mistakes kids make.

If that happens to you, don't get discouraged about it. It doesn't mean you're a horrible dad or that you have clumsier-than-normal kids. It means you need to create more mental and emotional margin for yourself. Don't book your schedule so full that you're constantly stressed out. Don't try to accomplish everything perfectly or in the next fifteen minutes. Take time to slow down, to be grateful, to laugh, to pray, to heal, to reset, to breathe.

2. CHOOSE RESILIENCE OVER CONTROL.

Let's be real. You're never fully "in control," even when things are going your way. When your baby has explosive diarrhea that shoots up their back and destroys the car seat thirty minutes into your well-planned road trip, you realize control is an illusion.

Instead of relying on control, develop resilience. Dads need to be like Bear Grylls: able to adapt and survive amid the harshest of circumstances. Rather than getting overwhelmed by things we didn't see coming, we need to dig deep. This is why we are here. It's why we are strong, why we're creative, why we've developed grit over the years. This is our moment to rise.

Resilience can be defined in different ways, but I see it as having at least three characteristics:

- the endurance to withstand pressure
- the elasticity to bounce back
- the flexibility to adapt

Those inflatable figures with weights at the bottom—the toys we used to have as kids—come to mind. No matter how hard you hit them, they'd pop back up, still smiling creepily at you.

Resilience is part mindset, part habit, part training, and part stubbornness. It's natural to humans, but it's also learned and developed. Think about it. Since our first day in this world—literally from the moment the birthing process starts—we've been squeezed and stretched and pushed into new places. Throughout our lives, every trial, every job, every problem builds iron into our souls.

As a father you'll need to engage all of that iron and more. Sometimes you will feel completely out of control and tempted to cave in. You might feel like running, quitting, or hiding. You might want to turn to an addiction or make a dumb decision. You might find yourself stressed, angry, or scared. Imposter syndrome or your inner bully might shout at you that you are the problem, you're not cut out for this, you'll never make it.

Those feelings are not the problem; we all have them at times. But what we do with them matters a whole lot. Truly resilient fathers know how to get up when they've been knocked down. They know how to survive, to endure, to bounce back, to pivot.

Resilience will always serve you better than control, and it's something you can choose at any time, in any circumstance.

3. DON'T CRY OVER SPILLED MILK . . . LITERALLY.

Recently we bought a trampoline for our yard. It came in two giant boxes that sat in my yard for weeks until the kids finally begged me enough to put it together. I didn't realize it was a two-person job or that a lot of people hire someone to put these things together for them. Supposedly Theo and Uriah were going to help me, but they got distracted and I got frustrated, so I ended up doing most of the job alone.

It was horrible. The thing had 108 springs that had to be attached to a wire frame, plus several legs that all had to go into the right slots at the right time. I'd get one leg in, and another would pop out. Also, I was building it on uneven ground—a big manufacturer no-no—and did I mention it was a sixteen-foot trampoline and this was during July in the desert? I just about lost my temper, my sanity, and my salvation on the same day. The kids had so much fun on it when I got it done, though, and I thought, *That was almost worth it.*

The next day I left for a three-day trip. My wife called me the first day. "Guess what?" she said, as if this was big news. "The trampoline has a hole in it."

"Babe," I said, "you should not have told me that. You should have just let me be happy in my ignorance until I got home."

She started laughing, then I started laughing. What I really wanted to do was set new records of anger, but I didn't. It wouldn't do any good. Sometimes you laugh so you don't descend into madness. To this day, nobody has confessed to making that hole. They try to pin the blame on the dog, who can't defend herself.

Don't cry over spilled milk, the saying goes. Kids will spill milk. They'll also spit milk up on your shirt, leave it out until it spoils, or put the completely empty carton back in the fridge. They're kids. That's what they do. You try to train and teach them, but at the end of the day, you can't control them—you can only control your response.

I've had to learn to have a mindset that laughs rather than cries when my kids mess up. It's probably helped that I usually make videos out of the crazy things that happen, so I try to see the (dark) humor in them, even while they're happening. I'll tell myself, *At least this is going to tell a great story*. It's morbid, but it calms me down.

Don't trip just because your kids are trying to figure out how to be human. When a baby throws up in your mouth, they're just as surprised as you. You get upset because it inconveniences your day or forces you to walk around with a soiled shirt, but they didn't plan that. They weren't aiming.

Think about how much a baby learns in just their first six months of life: their name, their parents' voices, how to control their hands enough to stick everything in their mouth, how to roll over and fall off things, how to laugh and cry and yell, how to start forming words, and so much more. It's all trial and error though. We know that, so we give them grace. We laugh at how cute they are as they try and fail and learn, and we let them take the time they need to develop.

DON'T TRIP JUST BECAUSE YOUR KIDS ARE TRYING TO FIGURE OUT HOW TO BE HUMAN.

The grace we give a baby is the same grace we need to give an eight-year-old. Obviously the bar is a lot higher, but being willing to extend patience and compassion to these humans-in-training is an essential part of fatherhood. There is so much they don't know, and that's not their fault. They're still learning.

I remember asking one of my kids, "How many times have I told you not to slam the door?" and he literally started trying to add up how many times I had told him that. He'd never heard the phrase before, and he assumed I was looking for a real number. In the middle of my frustration at the door-slamming, I had to laugh.

And then I had him practice quietly shutting the door a bunch of times, because I'm hoping that sooner or later muscle memory will kick in and he'll quit breaking the doorjamb.

Kids' brains are spinning a million miles an hour, trying to assimilate to an enormous, unfamiliar, overwhelming world. Every day, they're learning new words, new social skills, new character lessons, new facts. Their bodies are still growing, so of course they're going to trip or drop things. Their prefrontal cortex is still forming, so it's normal for them to be impulsive or make dumb choices sometimes. Their body is flooded with random hormones, so naturally they're going to act out once in a while—or every ten minutes.

I'm not making excuses for them by reminding myself of these things; I'm giving myself permission to extend grace rather than crying over spilled milk and broken trampolines.

4. GIVE YOURSELF GRACE.

It's crazy how often I find myself reacting to my kids the wrong way because my own insecurities were triggered somehow. I've realized that when I'm insecure, being a good dad is more difficult. Actually, in *Training Day*, Alonzo was a terrible dad. If his ego-driven, abusive voice is the one I'm listening to, it's going to come out in my parenting.

Part of eliminating insecurity is taking off the pressure to be perfect. I think we need to cut ourselves some slack as dads. I don't mean lowering our expectations of ourselves as much as I mean giving ourselves grace when we don't meet those expectations. It's a tricky balance. I know I'm too hard on myself sometimes, but I also know that if I mess up, it hurts my kids—which means I'd better do all I can not to mess up. I don't think I've fully figured out how to merge both of those realities.

It helps to remember that just as my kids are learning to be humans, I'm learning to be a dad. The process is ongoing, ever-changing. For over a decade, I've been learning to parent babies and small children. Currently, I'm figuring out how to parent preteens. Soon, I'll be learning to parent teenagers. After that, I'll be discovering how to parent young adults. I've learned a lot so far, but there is so much more I *don't* know. I'm committed to growing, though, which is what matters most.

It also helps to remember that each kid is different. Just because your first kid walked at a certain age, excels in school, or plays sports better than anyone on his team doesn't mean the second kid will. With each child, the learning process begins again. Give yourself grace as you get college degrees in all your kids.

One more thing: It gets more complex as they get older. That's another reason to keep giving yourself grace. The first year is really just about learning how to hold babies without dropping them. You feed them, change their diapers, and in general just keep them alive. Then they start walking and talking—and they never sit down or shut up again. Each new stage is more complicated (and expensive) than the last.

As they get older your goal is still "don't drop them." Except now, you're not concerned about dropping them physically but rather dropping them emotionally. You don't want to drop the connection with them and the safety you provide as they keep growing and learning. No matter how tall they get, how much hair grows out of random places, how much funk emanates from their body, or how long it takes them to tell a story, they still need you close. They need you to see their struggles and meet their needs, and that's what you were built by God to do.

We will just keep getting better at this. I really believe that. The mistakes will be outweighed by the successes; the errors will lead to learning. We'll be better dads, better husbands, better friends, better employees, better bosses, better neighbors.

The next time you're talking with a father-to-be, don't just share all your horror stories. Sure, tell him they will throw up in his mouth, and tell him what to do about it. But most of all, tell him he's going to be the father he needs to be. He's enough for the job.

Part Number

LEGACY

Title

Start

Kids are the ultimate legacy because the investment you make in them will bear fruit for generations to come. Legacy isn't about fame or ego but about what you leave behind. It's a reflection of what you valued enough to invest in. Legacy is about the satisfaction that comes from knowing your investment will keep having a return even when you are gone.

Legacy takes work, but it's good work, and it's work God created you to do. This is the topic of **chapter 5, "The Biggest Stage You'll Stand On."** Here, we explore the idea that you are collaborating with God on a masterpiece.

One thing our kids will carry with them forever is the voice we instill in their heads. **Chapter 6, "The Voice They Need to Hear,"** is about helping our kids have the right voice: one infused with confidence, wisdom, and love.

THE BIGGEST STAGE YOU'LL STAND ON

Start

As I've said already, before I became a stay-at-home dad in 2015, I was a rapper and hip-hop performer. I would write and record songs, and I'd tour for a week or two each month. I was proud of the money I was making, but since we had to pay for childcare when I was on tour, I knew I needed to make more.

I remember asking Yvette, "How much would we need to make a month to make this work? Ten thousand?"

She said, "Nah."

"Twenty?"

"No."

"Fifty thousand?"

"Nope."

"How much then?"

She replied, "Basically what you're asking is how much money it would take to turn me into a single mom, because that's what I feel like when you leave."

I thought, _Welp, that hurt, but at least she's on brand . . . Okay, this career isn't going to work in the long run._

Her comment stuck with me. Was my dream really to stand on bigger and brighter stages, all in the name of ministry, money, or influence? Because what Yvette wanted—and what my kids needed—was more of my presence, not more of my money.

When I did shows, I'd travel around the country, gathering crowds, getting people jumping, and putting on performances from the stage. It was fulfilling, but it was also temporary. The high lasted only a moment.

As I thought about how much my presence meant to my kids, I realized something: The biggest stage I will ever stand on is my living room, and my most important audience is my own children. That's where my effort will have the greatest impact, where my message will make the biggest difference. It's one thing to entertain an audience for an hour or two, but that can't compare to fighting imaginary bad guys with my son on a Saturday morning and creating memories that will last a lifetime.

Soon after that, I went from being a traveling hip-hop entertainer to a creative stay-at-home dad, and it was the best decision I ever made. I still did music on the side, but it stopped being my top priority and turned into more of a side hustle. From there the fatherhood channels took off, and now, ironically, I'm on a bigger stage than I probably could have hoped for had I made music my priority—*and* I'm home most of the time.

I don't share this so you'll quit your job and stay home with your kids, especially if you're the primary breadwinner. For us, that decision was made after a lot of hard, late-night conversations and soul-searching. I'm sharing my story because I want you to see how important you are. Regardless of your career choice or schedule, the greatest influence you ever have will be on your children. Your living room is your biggest stage, and your kids are your most important fans.

As fathers we don't often recognize how much influence we have. Someone asked me recently why I developed such a passion for talking about fatherhood, and I told him it was partly because I don't think my dad understood how valuable he was to me as a kid. Too many dads don't realize they are on a stage every day, giving the performance of their lives for the most precious and impressionable audience imaginable. They don't know the biggest camera lenses are their kids' eyes, eyes that are always watching, learning, imitating, growing.

That should encourage you, not scare you. Your sacrifice matters. Your effort is going to pay off. The blood, sweat, and tears you pour into your children are investments that will pay huge dividends in the future. Yes, it's a lot of work, but it's your greatest work, and it's a good work.

FATHERHOOD IS GOOD WORK

One time I took Theo to an Anaheim Ducks hockey game for his birthday. I probably shouldn't have done it because we were going through a tough season financially, and the tickets were crazy expensive—but the Ducks were playing the Oilers, which is Theo's favorite team. We were in the nosebleeds, so high up that we felt like we were going to tip over when we stood up. Even though the Oilers lost, Theo loved it. The crowds, the noise, the fights—it was great.

As we were leaving, he wanted to find a jersey for his favorite player, Connor McDavid. This was Anaheim, so of course they didn't have it. He asked if I'd buy it for him online for his birthday. I said yes, but then I looked up how much they cost, and I almost choked. I had to break my promise and tell him we couldn't afford it. Naturally, he got mad. He couldn't understand why I'd go back on my word. He kept saying I had promised, so I had to do it.

As a dad, that felt terrible. Insecurity started to shoot up inside me because, once again, I felt inadequate. The temptation was to snap at him in self-defense. After all, he didn't know how hard it had been to leave work early, travel to pick him up, and drive to Anaheim. He didn't know his brother had wanted to go, but I was forced to say no because I couldn't afford another ticket.

Instead of lashing out during the ninety-minute trip home, we had an honest conversation. I explained to him that we weren't in a good place financially. I told him the trip and the game had been expensive, and we had to make tough choices. He's a smart, empathetic kid, and he understood. He even apologized.

That convo wasn't easy. The game itself was fun, but the whole jersey thing was *work*. It took work to keep my temper and overcome my insecurity. It took work to explain our situation and give him context. All of it was messy and vulnerable. But it was *necessary* work, and it was *good* work.

I think I handled the situation well that time, but there have been plenty of other times when I haven't done the good work and instead have opted for the "easy" way out: usually by losing my cool or just shutting someone down. I'm learning that good fatherhood is often about being willing to put in the work.

Here's the thing: *That's our role.* We shouldn't expect applause and accolades from our kids for simply doing our job as fathers.

Someday, probably when they have kids of their own, they'll recognize at least some of what we did for them. But for now they are pretty much oblivious to it—just as we were when we were kids.

Sometimes I hear people complaining about how much they've done for their kids: all the sacrifices they made and the hard things they had to do. They wear the grind of parenting like a badge of martyrdom. "I gave up so much. I did all this for you." Yes, parenting is challenging at times. We can all agree on that. Nobody likes being woken up eight times in one night or driving four hours a day just to shuttle kids back and forth. What bothers me, though, is when we let an underlying attitude of "you owe me" creep in.

The attitude I want to have toward my kids is that their well-being and success is a central goal for me—not out of obligation, and not with resentment, but simply because they are my kids. A huge part of my life is for them. All I have is theirs, and I am committed to caring for them. They don't "owe" me anything because they didn't choose to be born; Yvette and I chose that for them. Now we have the privilege of sowing our lives into them. To call our role a sacrifice is to sell it short. This is not a sacrifice; it's an investment. It's a privilege. It's family.

Family is a completely different category of people from the rest of the world. Sometimes Yvette will tell me, "Babe, you're my favorite person." She's being sweet, but I can't stand it. I'll be like, "I wasn't aware there was a competition. I mean, I'm glad I rank at the top, but who's coming in second? How far behind are they? Should I be worried?"

I don't even think that way. For me, my wife and kids are in a different category from the rest of the world. They are not my favorites—they are my onlys. That's why giving all I can for them is not a sacrifice but rather the logical, obvious result of being a family unit.

I think the term *hard* is the wrong word to use when it comes to fatherhood. *Hard* implies gritting your teeth and making sacrifices, even though you'd rather not. There is no hope built into the term *hard*—just pain, sweat, and subtle regret.

That's why *work* is a better term. Parenting is work, and it works if you work it. We were designed for this, after all. Our bodies and minds are built to do good work. The Bible says, "For we are God's handiwork, created in Christ Jesus to do good works, which God prepared in advance for us to do" (Ephesians 2:10). Rather than viewing the difficult moments of fatherhood as hard, view them as the good works God has prepared for you. Putting trampolines together is good work. Wiping runny noses and cleaning butts is good work. Stepping on Lego pieces in the dark is good work. Trying to figure out who left a turd in the toilet is good work. Answering incessant questions is good work.

Back when I was touring, I'd do whatever it took to have a great show. I'd get up early, stay up late, put in fourteen-hour days, eat terrible food, and more. How much more should I be willing to do for my family, my biggest stage?

Aspects of parenting have really gotten under my skin at times, and I've wanted to say to myself, "Don't complain, Glen. Just do it." And that might work, at least for a time. I've learned, though, that if I take a couple of steps back and change my heart, I can choose how I want to feel. I can say, "Wow, what a privilege I have. I *get* to be a father. I *get* to raise these kids."

Don't settle for viewing fatherhood as a necessary evil or a cross to bear. It's a gift. It's a privilege. You and I are doing good work, bredren, and it is going to produce good fruit. Why? Because we're laboring together with God to create masterpieces.

COLLABORATING ON MASTERPIECES

I've watched people build clay sculptures before, and often they start off with just a wire on a hook. They add a piece of clay, then another, letting the clay mold together until eventually a face takes shape.

That's how parenting feels to me. You have a piece of clay, and you're continuously adding to it. You form and shape it to the best of your ability. At some point, though, the sculpture takes on a life of its own. It starts telling you what it's going to be. The sculpture might even take a piece off and say, "I don't need this part." As a parent, you've got to be okay with that. You stand back and watch as the masterpiece works on itself.

A sculpture that is being molded is pliable, but that means it's also delicate. An artist has to provide a safe, healthy, controlled environment for the sculpture to become what it's becoming. The sculpture wouldn't let just anyone come near its wet clay. In the same way, our children need to be protected as they grow. They need a safe, controlled home environment and family system.

It's the most beautiful collab: God does the bulk of the work, and they make choices along the way, but as fathers and parents, we have the joy of being intimately involved with every step. That's why they end up looking like us—for better or for worse. Not just in their physical features but in their attitudes, vocabulary, sense of humor, and actions.

Your children are the greatest piece of art you will ever create. They are the greatest project you'll ever put your hand to and the most enduring legacy you could ever leave behind. Your kids will be forever changed because you are present in their lives.

The knowledge that you are collaborating with the Creator of the entire universe to raise your kids should do two things. First, it should give you room to breathe. God's not just helping you; he's leading the way, and his grace is enough for you. Second, it should add value to what you are doing. It's far too easy to devalue what you do, to limit your role to just protecting, providing, teaching, or disciplining. That's part of the job, but what you are doing is much deeper and formative than that. You are creating a masterpiece together with God.

While the knowledge and training we impart verbally is helpful, most of the impact we have comes from our presence. Who we are will always speak louder than what we say. How we treat our wives, how we handle stress, how we apologize when we're wrong, how we laugh and enjoy life—these are the things that will get deep into our kids' beings and give them a vision for how they can live. Through our presence and our interactions, we are reproducing ourselves not just physically but emotionally, relationally, spiritually, and mentally.

That's why it's so important to continually father ourselves, as we discussed earlier. I'm convinced the most challenging part of fatherhood is putting in the "good work" to heal our wounds and become healthier versions of ourselves. If we do that, we progressively heal each generation rather than progressively scarring them. When Theo called me out for not buying him a jersey, I had to do some quick work on *myself* before I could have the right conversation with him. I had to make sure I was seeing myself the right way rather than letting shame or inadequacy take over.

In a very real sense, when you parent your children, you end up parenting yourself. Not only are you collaborating on masterpieces called your kids but you're also letting God continue to sculpt the masterpiece called *you*.

IN ALL LABOR THERE IS PROFIT

I was meeting with my men's small group one time, and we started talking about parenting. I made this offhand comment: "I don't know one dude who wants to be like his dad. I can't think of a single person who would say that."

Several of the other guys agreed with me, but a friend named Phil said, "Man, if I could be half the man my dad is, I would be successful."

We all looked at him and said, "Word?"

He said, "Yeah, man, I would be. My dad was honorable to my mom. He was a great father. He stayed at home. He did my sister's hair. He played with us."

I was blown away by that. My wife and I know Phil's dad from church. His name is Mike, and he's been a mentor for us. So the next time I saw Mike, I walked up to him and said, "Hey, man, just so you know, I was talking to Phil the other day, and I was saying I don't know anybody who wants to be like their dad. And Phil said if he can be half the dad you are, he'll be a success."

Mike is one of those dudes whose face you can't read when you're talking to him, so I didn't know what was coming. All of a sudden, he started crying. Not just little tears, either, but snot-bubble sobs right there in front of me. He was so moved that his son had that opinion of him. It was as if he was seeing the return on his investment over all those years.

The sight moved me. I'll never forget that reaction. When I talk to Mike now, I ask him about parenting. I want to know what he instilled in his three children and how he lives as a father. What values did he teach? How did he live his life within the home? I want to learn what he did right because I want that same return on investment in my own children.

Earlier I mentioned that fatherhood is good work. *Work* should lead to *reward*. That's the whole point; it's meant to accomplish something over the long term. Proverbs says, "All hard work brings a profit, but mere talk leads only to poverty" (14:23). The great thing about the work of fatherhood is that your investment will bring a return that lasts for generations.

The primary "profit" of parenting is the health and well-being of your children as they grow into adulthood. The effort you put into your children is directly responsible not just for their survival but also for their development and growth into the people God has created them to be. That's an insane privilege and a serious calling.

You might not see the results of your investment yet, but the effort you're putting into your kids—your masterpieces—*will* have an effect. I believe they will not only grow up to be the people God designed them to be but they'll also honor and love you. They'll want you in their lives. They'll keep learning from you, and they'll teach you too. Then, they'll reproduce what you've done in the next generation. Fatherhood is an investment that keeps on creating a profit; it's a seed that never stops bearing fruit.

MAKE IT A PRIORITY

Pat, the pastor and mentor I mentioned earlier who has seven daughters, is an incredible athlete. A couple of years ago, he was competing in an Ironman race, and he got in a terrible accident. He was hit by a car and ended up fighting for his life. When I found out about it, I immediately flew out to where he was to be with him in the hospital.

Over the next few days, we had a lot of time to talk. The thing I remember most is how passionate he was about spending more time with his family. He almost felt guilty for having invested so much energy into his physical training during the previous four years. He kept telling me that he just wanted his family to be close to him, to live in his home or be together on their property.

Keep in mind, we're not talking about an absentee father here. Pat is a guy who loves his family and has always been around them, so hearing his passion to be even closer to them had a deep impact on me. He had come face-to-face with death, and all that mattered was family.

Watching Pat's desire to be close to his family is one of the reasons we decided to move to a farm with more land as well as buy an RV. I feel a sense of urgency around connecting with my kids and building a relationship with them now, while they are young. I want my family close; I want to be there for them, and I want them to be with me.

When we catch a glimpse of how valuable and powerful our fatherhood role is, we feel a sense of urgency about it. If this is our biggest stage, it needs to be a top priority in our lives. If we're going to be the fathers our kids need, we've got to make sure the craziness and chaos of life that pulls us in a thousand different directions doesn't distract us from our families.

That's an ongoing challenge, and you need self-compassion in the middle of it because you'll often feel like you're not enough for all the demands placed on you. The struggle is real, but the struggle is also important. It forces you to choose what really matters. There will be times when something has to give, when you'll have to cheat something—but make sure it's not always your family that gives in or gets cheated. If you're going to err, err on the side of spending too much time with your family. Err on the side of laughing too much, of enjoying them too deeply, of closing the laptop too soon, and of going on bike rides too often. Not because you have to but because you *want* to and because you know how valuable your presence is to them.

IF YOU'RE GOING TO ERR, ERR ON THE SIDE OF SPENDING TOO MUCH TIME WITH YOUR FAMILY.

quote

The Bible says, "Let us not become weary in doing good, for at the proper time we will reap a harvest if we do not give up" (Galatians 6:9). I don't know what the "proper" time is— that's in God's hands. But I do know his grace is enough for us. He gives us the strength to keep doing good works, to keep building masterpieces, to keep playing to the audience that is our children, until his perfect time comes. Yes, family and fatherhood are work sometimes, but they are the best work we could possibly do.

06

Chapter Number

THE VOICE THEY NEED TO HEAR

Title

— Start

've started hiking for exercise, and recently Uriah, my second oldest, asked to go with me on my usual hike because he said he wanted to get in better shape. "Are you sure?" I asked. "It's a five-mile trail with some steep hills, and it's hot out there."

He insisted, "I can do it! I know I can."

Now, I know my son, and I'm aware he has a very high view of what he is capable of, which is something I love. But he also tends to give up quickly. Sure enough, partway through the hike, the excitement wore off and the heat and fatigue kicked in—as did all the feels. He's dramatic, which seems to run in my family, so I had to spend the next hour encouraging him. Since we were in the desert, we had no cell service; it wasn't like I could call an Uber to come pick us up. And I sure wasn't going to carry him out.

"I can't do this," he kept saying.

"Yes, you can," I'd reply. "You're strong."

"No, I'm weak. I'm hot. I'm tired."

"You can do it."

"What if I pass out?"

"Well, you'll wake up."

He literally fell over at one point. He just collapsed and started crying. I had to talk him through that too. "I promise you, you've got this. This is the hardest part, then it gets way easier."

It was a huge learning experience. Not just for him but for me. Together, we went through all the cycles of fear and frustration that each of us experiences when we attempt to do hard things.

I finally got on his case a little bit over the way he was talking about himself. He kept saying, "I can't do this. I'm too weak. I'm going to die."

"Yes, you can do it," I said. "You gotta stop talking like that. Your inner voice needs to be positive."

Then he told me, "I just need a hug right now."

That was both beautiful and disgusting, because we were sweating like nobody's business. I was like, "Really? Why do you need a hug right now?"

He didn't know. He just knew he needed one in order to keep going. So we stood there in the middle of the desert heat, my man-boobs pressed against his man-boobs, and hugged until he felt better and was able to keep going.

Obviously, he didn't die. He didn't pass out either. When he finished the hike, he was very proud of himself, and I was proud of him too. I asked him, "If you could go back and talk to yourself during that hike, what would you say to encourage yourself?"

He thought for a second. "I can do it. Push harder."

I loved that answer so much. I could literally hear him silencing the bully in his head. He was replacing "I can't do this" with "I *can* do this." When things get tough, instead of saying, "Give up now," he was reminding himself to say, "Push harder."

I made a video out of the experience and posted it on our channel. Naturally I got a few angry comments because everybody hates to see a little boy suffer. Even my wife said, "Babe, why didn't you call me?" Inside I was thinking, *Because you would have let him quit*. But all I said was "No cell service."

As a father, I hated to see him suffer too. But even if I could have called a helicopter to airlift us out of there, quitting wasn't what my son needed—or what he really *wanted*. The experience was so much bigger than surviving a five-mile hike. It was about seeing himself differently and learning that he really can achieve what he wants to do, even if things feel overwhelming in the moment. He can dream big things *and* do big things.

NURTURE, NOT CONTROL

Fatherhood is not pretty. It's messy business sometimes. It's dramatic business. It's sweaty-hugs-in-the-hot-desert business. That is part of our role though. We will often know what our kids are capable of even better than they do, and if we are willing to stay by their side and encourage them, we can help them grow into the people they were created by God to be. As fathers, we are mentors, teachers, coaches, and cheerleaders. We come alongside our kids to protect and serve them as they blossom and develop.

Don't get me wrong here. This is not about running a boot camp or demanding perfection. Nor is it about ignoring your kids' feelings or trying to force them into some preconceived idea you might have of what they should be. There have been plenty of times when I've let Uriah back out of something, and that's okay. But this time, he needed to finish.

Fatherhood is less about control and more about *nurture*. Your goal is to help them step into the fullness of their potential. You don't even know what that potential is yet, but you catch glimpses, and then you nudge them in the right direction as they keep growing.

Farm life is relatively new to us, but there are two things that are clear about any living thing. First, it will take its own sweet time growing; and second, it will grow up to be what it was designed to be. I can't force a tree, plant, or flower to develop faster or differently than its inner design dictates. Sure, I can decide where to plant it and guide its growth a little bit, but my role is mostly to nourish and protect it during its built-in, God-designed growth process.

In a similar way, as a father, your role is not to control, force, or impose your idea of who your kids should be on them. God has put a lot in them, but it's in seed form. Your job is to come alongside them and do whatever they need done in order to bring those things to life. God is doing the hard work of creating growth, and if you pay attention, your kids will show you what they need and who they are becoming. You are there to protect, provide, encourage, and teach as that future becomes reality.

We have more influence on how our kids turn out than we do on the trees or bushes in our yard. But ultimately, as I said before, we need to diminish so they can increase. They're going to want to cut off their locs or wear certain styles of clothing, and it's important for us to discern when it's time to start letting them make the decisions that are so important for their identity and confidence.

By "nurturing," I don't mean just hugs, bedtime stories, and compliments. Those are part of the package, but nurturing includes whatever they need to grow. Sometimes nurturing looks like telling your child that if he passes out during a hike, he'll wake up. Other times it looks like driving them back and forth to hockey practice even when it means working late into the night to meet a deadline. Other times it looks like a heart-to-heart conversation or making them do chores or chasing them around the room pretending to be a superhero or sitting with them when they're sick even though you'd rather be chasing their mother around your own bedroom. No matter what form nurture takes, the desired outcome is the healthy development of your children.

As dads, I think we sometimes confuse these two concepts of nurture and control. If we're not careful, we can focus too much on getting them to do what we want and too little on getting them to do what they need. The difference between the two lies in the motive behind them. When we're encouraging or even requiring our kids to do something, we've got to make sure it's for them, not for us. Both nurture and control mean being highly involved in their lives, but only nurture is capable of releasing and empowering over the long haul—and that's what they truly need.

When I say "highly involved," I mean it. Fatherhood is a contact sport. These kids sleep in your home, eat your food, wipe boogers on your wall, and put holes in your trampoline. You *must* be involved in their development and growth. That's why they call you dad, and it's why they usually carry your last name.

So if this involvement doesn't look like ironfisted control, what does it look like? It looks like *showing* them how to live and *telling* them what they need to know.

SHOW AND TELL

When creating videos, there are two main elements that work together: showing and telling. "Showing" involves imagery, such as the shots, the location, the lighting, and the action. "Telling" primarily involves dialogue. It's what people say to each other or to the camera. The best videos have both showing and telling, and the two elements together tell a powerful story.

In the same way, when you're raising your kids, you want to have a mixture of showing and telling. Remember, their eyes are the biggest cameras, and they're always watching (sometimes from dark hallways after they're supposed to be in bed). The goal is for both your example in the home (actions) and your teaching and encouragement (words) to work together to give them guidance and support. Let's look at a couple of ways to do each of these.

WHAT SHOULD YOU SHOW THEM?

The list of things you might *show* them is infinite because kids are sponges who soak up everything you say and do—especially things like the cuss words you didn't mean for them to learn. Human behavior is mostly caught, not taught, and they catch it first and foremost from you.

That could either freak you out or inspire you to be intentional about what you show them, or maybe a bit of both. They'll pick up some things you'll wish they hadn't, but more than that, they'll pick up the things you take the time and energy to show them. That's encouraging, especially when they're not listening to your words because they're running around screaming like they're possessed. They're still watching your actions and learning from your example. That gives you a lot of freedom and power as a dad.

The specific things you show them are up to you, and they'll likely include your unique areas of expertise. My kids know a lot about filming and social media, for example, but I haven't taught them anything about how to rebuild an engine. (I don't even know what that means.) Generally speaking, here are three things to focus on:

1. Show them what is normal, right, and good.

Long before our kids are unleashed on the world, they will have been learning from us what it means to be human. That's the "biggest stage" idea we talked about in the last chapter. In the home and with their family, children learn what is normal, what is expected, and what is right. As fathers, our actions and reactions will teach them how to carry themselves, whether we realize it or not.

That's a scary but important truth. In my home, my kids learn that it's normal to treat their siblings with respect. It's normal for Dad and Mom to love each other. It's normal to walk through the kitchen rather than running. It's normal to laugh a lot. It's normal to work hard and play hard. It's normal (and nonnegotiable) to wipe your butt after using the toilet. It's normal for me to expect that I shouldn't have to smell you to figure out whether you put on deodorant, because you love yourself and the rest of us enough to not let us smell you like that.

Healthy mindsets and habits are also modeled more than they are taught. Every day, you are showing your kids how to be well-balanced, decent human beings who act with common sense, good manners, and intelligence. You are imparting the wisdom and life lessons you've picked up over the years, which are invaluable gifts that help set them up for success.

2. Show them what is possible.

Not only are they learning how to be humans; they are also learning how to become like you. While they won't want to be exactly like you (especially once the teen years roll around), you are their hero, and they look up to you. Long before they've thought about college or a career choice, you represent what they can expect to achieve and become.

- On a **family** level, show them what a marriage and family can look like. Be the best family you can be because they're going to reproduce what they see. When they are grown and gone, they'll have that solid example to look back on, and the bar will be set high.

- On a **personal** level, show them how to continually grow and mature. Let them see an example of genuine love, someone who knows how to treat people with generosity and empathy. Be an adult who is both confident and humble, able to stand up for yourself but also able to work with others with grace and patience.

- On a **relational** level, let them see the value of a wider community. They'll learn social skills from you, and they'll discover how to have a wide world. They'll also learn safety and boundaries. They'll watch how you choose friends who share your values and add to your life.

- On a **work** and **financial** level, model a good work ethic and financial responsibility. Many of us are not where we want to be in this area, but we're on a journey, and it's good for our kids to be part of the journey. They can learn how to work hard, save, budget, spend wisely—and how to enjoy their blessings and be generous to others.

- Finally, on a **spiritual** level, show them how to know God. Help them see what it means to trust God and live in wisdom and love. By your example, teach them to pray, to read the Bible, and to value the church community.

Never underestimate the power of simply doing life in front of your kids. When you grow in an area, when you set and accomplish a goal, when you make healthy changes, when you take steps forward—each victory is a source of vision and inspiration for your kids.

3. Show them how to recover from mistakes.

I hate that this is true, but you will mess up in front of your kids at times. You'll lose your temper, you'll say things you didn't mean, you'll make decisions that don't work out, you'll hurt their feelings, and you'll embarrass yourself or them.

That sucks—but it also offers an invaluable opportunity. They are watching your every move, and if you only model perfection, how are they supposed to measure up to that? That facade sets the bar too high. It isn't realistic or honest, because we all know that behind the scenes, we're painfully fallible.

NEVER UNDERESTIMATE THE POWER OF SIMPLY DOING LIFE IN FRONT OF YOUR KIDS.

quote

You can keep up the hero-who-never-messes-up persona for the first few years of their lives, but the image starts to crack as they grow older and become more aware of the realities of life. *Let it crack.* Let them see your humanity. But don't stop there. Show them how you deal with your mistakes.

What should you model? Here are a few things that spring to mind, and I'm sure you could add a few more from your own experience of being a flawed (aka normal) human being.

- Model **grace**: Have compassion and patience with yourself.
- Model **humility**: Admit your flaws and be willing to ask for help.
- Model a **growth mindset**: Seek ways to improve and grow rather than repeating mistakes.
- Model **emotional intelligence**: Let them see how you

process frustration, embarrassment, and anxiety, and how you move from there to a place of stability.

- Model **resilience**: Show them how to bounce back, stand up under pressure, and move forward even when things didn't work out like you planned.

Often we don't even realize we're teaching them these things. We're simply putting our life skills into practice and doing our best to survive and move forward. But they're learning lessons, including *It's okay to cry when I'm sad. It's okay to feel hurt; I will get through it, and life will be good again. It's okay to be frustrated, as long as I don't punch the person I'm mad at.*

Over the years, they'll pick up hundreds—perhaps thousands—of invaluable life lessons that we impart through example.

We won't be perfect at this, which means we also get to model how to apologize, make amends, and grow. This is vital to the process. Don't expect your kids to be perfect, and don't expect yourself to be perfect either. The unfortunate truth is that they will often learn more from your mistakes than from your successes. On the flip side, the beautiful truth is that they won't have to make those same mistakes. By being open and honest, you're teaching them how to both avoid those specific errors and—even more importantly—how to recover from errors they'll make down the road. As I've said, fatherhood is messy, so let them see the messiness, but also model the process you use to work through the mess and get better at what you do.

WHAT SHOULD YOU TELL THEM?

Telling goes hand in hand with showing. At key moments in your fathering journey, your words will deeply impact your kids. It's hard to plan for those moments, because kids seem to sense when you're about to drop a profound life lesson and choose that moment to start a video game or knock over their drink. But if you are ready to talk when they are ready to hear, you can change the course of their life—or at least their day—with just a few words.

Paul told Timothy, "Preach the word; be prepared in season and out of season; correct, rebuke and encourage—with great patience and careful instruction" (2 Timothy 4:2). He might as well have been talking to fathers. Not that you're going to literally "preach" at them, because nobody likes to be sermonized at, but this idea of being ready at any moment to correct, rebuke, or encourage as needed—and to do it with patience and care—is a perfect description of your teaching role with your kids.

It's worth mentioning that the timetable for this instruction is usually up to them. They often want to talk when you're in the middle of a project, behind on a deadline, on the toilet, or trying to go to bed. While you can't *always* drop everything and attend to them, you *often* can, and you'll probably never regret doing it.

So what should you tell them? Again, the list should be very personal since you have a unique archive of lessons learned and skills acquired over the years. But in general, focus on these two things:

1. Tell them who they are.

Our kids are loved, unique, called, courageous, intelligent, powerful, and so much more. That is how God sees them, and it's how we see them, and it's how they should see themselves. (They are also loud, stubborn, smelly, and a few other adjectives, but those aren't the ones we should focus on.)

They probably don't see themselves in a positive light as much as they should—just as you and I don't see ourselves that way—because life has a way of beating up on our self-worth. As a dad, you can help counteract the negative voices around them by speaking life. Proverbs says, "The tongue has the power of life and death, and those who love it will eat its fruit" (18:21).

There is a lot you can't control about their lives, but the words they hear from you are completely up to you. Your words are like a fatherhood superpower that wields incredible influence on how they see themselves and what they believe they can accomplish. Psychology talks about the importance of something called self-efficacy, which is a person's belief that they are able, sufficient, and adequate for a challenge. Studies show that the more we see ourselves as capable, the more capable we are. Self-efficacy begins to form in our brains in early childhood, and parents play a huge role in that.

Don't just tell them what to do; tell them who they are. What they do is important, but who they are is foundational to the rest of their lives. Be intentional about speaking words that shape their self-view, that help them see themselves as you see them and as God sees them.

2. Tell them what they need to know.

I mentioned that one of my kids used to slam the door. All day, every day. I always knew when he entered or exited because nobody else made the entire house shake like that. He broke the doorjamb at least three times.

I'd say, "Don't slam the door!" And he'd ask, "Why not?"

That was a valid question, but the truth is, I didn't want to take the time to explain it. Plus, I knew it would lead to a bunch more

questions. If I said, "Because it makes the door weak," he'd say, "Why is that bad? What might happen?"

"Somebody might break in."

"But you said we live in a safe community."

"Yes, but sometimes there are bad people."

"How do we know if they are good or bad?"

quote

DON'T JUST TELL THEM WHAT TO DO; TELL THEM WHO THEY ARE.

It would never end. I just wanted the door closed softly, and I wanted to be able to focus on my work. His curiosity was valid, though, and I had to balance telling him what to do and not do with teaching him why it was important.

There are times to tell your kids, "Because I said so," but that should be a last resort, such as when you can tell they've moved from inquisitiveness to defiance. Telling them what to do has value, but giving them the *why* behind the *what* helps them apply their learning across a much wider horizon of possible events. You're giving them not just facts but reasoning, common sense, values, and worldview.

"What they need to know" is infinite, of course. You have only a few years with them, so you can't teach them every possible thing. My suggestion is to be intentional about communicating top-level things like safety, spiritual truths, money management, how to treat people, and how to resolve conflict, but to do so in an organic way as situations arise. You'll rarely sit them down in front of a whiteboard or create a PowerPoint deck to teach a lesson (although I have done that a few times). Instead, you'll take advantage of teaching moments that arise during the day.

Of course, since these teaching moments are not planned, they don't always happen when you're in the best mood. Sometimes you have to father yourself real quickly so you can be in the right head-space to teach your kids something. If they're fighting like cats and dogs, for example, it's tempting to show up with fire and brimstone just to put an end to the noise; but that might not be what they really need. Maybe they need a firm voice at first so they stop beating each other up, then a calm, mature voice to help them sort through their emotions and grow in their self-control.

The more knowledge and wisdom they gain as kids, the more success they're likely to have later on. As a dad, you get to impart what you've learned by telling them what they need to know.

THE VOICE IN THEIR HEADS

When it comes to our mentoring role as fathers, I've saved the most important point for last. Recently someone asked me the same question I asked my circle of friends back when I was about to be a father: "What are the things you want to teach your kids?" Remember, back then I thought learning to fight was going to be high on the priority list, but I was wrong. Now, four kids and over a decade later, my answer was quick and confident: "I want to teach them to have the right voice in their heads."

Yes, I want to teach them to have a good work ethic, to manage their money well, to stay healthy, to choose good friends, and a million other things. But the one thing that stands out to me more than probably anything else is their inner sense of confidence and self-esteem.

I've had to work diligently on changing my inner voice. I've learned the hard way just how powerful those whispers of insecurity, inadequacy, and fear can be. When I was nineteen, I was on the verge of committing suicide, and it was because I had spent too long listening to a hateful, hopeless voice. I am committed to putting a different voice in my kids' minds, one that will encourage them and uplift them. I don't want them to grow up listening to a bully in their brains. That's the reason I reminded Uriah to change his inner voice on that desert hike, and it's in my mind every time I praise them, push them, and champion them.

This world is a crazy, often cruel place, and there will be no shortage of voices trying to influence our kids to see themselves negatively. I live and work in the social media world, and believe me, it has never been easier to find ways to feel bad about ourselves. Our kids face an uphill battle to develop positive self-talk.

That's why the home is so important. As parents, we can't control the world outside, and there's only so much we can do to limit its influence as our kids grow up. But we can control the atmosphere of the home. We can decide what words, tone, and messaging our kids receive from the most important people in their world: their family.

As I've mentioned, if we don't father ourselves in this area, we'll talk to our kids the way we talk to ourselves. Maybe not when they're small, but as they get older, it's going to spill out. I still have a long way to go in this area. If I want my kids to have the right voice in their heads, I need to make sure I'm listening to the right voice in my own head.

That day on the hike, I recognized the voice my son was hearing: the tone, the language, the emotion. It's the voice I often hear mocking me in my own head. I've learned to fight it though. I've found strategies to retrain it, to recalibrate it, to replace it. That's what I want my kids to learn too.

In the Bible James talked quite a bit about the power of the tongue. One thing he said always stands out in my mind: "With the tongue we praise our Lord and Father, and with it we curse human beings, who have been made in God's likeness. Out of the same mouth come praise and cursing. My brothers and sisters, this should not be. Can both fresh water and salt water flow from the same spring?" (3:9–11).

James was speaking about how we talk to other people, but I think the principle first needs to be applied to how we speak *to* ourselves and *about* ourselves. Do we "curse" ourselves, even though we were made in God's image? Or do we value who we are and who we are becoming?

From there, we need to consistently speak positive words *to* our kids and *about* our kids, and we need to teach them to do the same toward themselves. They also are made in the image of God. Our words and actions need to be focused on training that inner voice to bless, not curse. When the time comes for them to move out and create their own lives, I want them to hear my voice in their heads, speaking far louder than condemnation, anxiety, or doubt.

The best way I know how to do that is to keep working on this cycle of fathering myself and fathering them. As I grow, I teach them; as I teach them, they grow; as they grow, they teach me; and so the cycle continues.

In the journey called fatherhood, you can't give up. You can't call an Uber or a helicopter to skip over the hard parts. Instead, you walk through them, sweat and dirt and hugs and all. You tell yourself, "I can do this. Push harder. Don't quit. I am enough for this task. I am the father my kids need."

As you do, your kids watch you, learn from you, and grow better because of you. You are their hero, and even your imperfections are being changed and redeemed by God. You can be confident that your influence and investment in their lives will bear fruit for generations to come.

04

ENGAGING

Start

Fatherhood is a contact sport. You can't raise your kids from a distance. If you want to understand who they are, see their needs, and help them grow, you have to meet them where they are. That will look different with each child and in each season, but the goal is always the same: connecting, engaging, and being present.

One of the most obvious—and fun—ways to do this is simply to play with them. That comes naturally to children, but as fathers, sometimes we have to work at it a little. In **chapter 7, "Becoming Childish Again,"** we look at what play looks like and why it's so important.

Next, in **chapter 8, "The Gift of Presence,"** we talk about how valuable our presence is in our kids' lives. Amid the hustle and chaos of life, it's easy to forget that what our kids want the most from us really isn't that complicated: They just need us to be there for them.

Chapter Number

BECOMING CHILDISH AGAIN

Title

Start

Years ago, when the two oldest boys were still very young, we lived in a condo that was essentially an apartment in Vista, California, a suburb of San Diego. One day the boys were chasing each other around in capes, pretending to fight bad guys. There was an extra cape, and spontaneously I put it on and took the kids outside. We spent the next hour yelling and running all over that apartment complex, fighting imaginary villains. It was a memorable moment for me because I realized I honestly didn't care that the whole world could see me making a fool of myself. I was playing with my kids. I wasn't just being child-like; I was *childish* in the best possible meaning of the word. The boys loved it, and I did too.

I don't think I would have even had the concept of playing that way with my kids had it not been for Mr. Hale, the dad of my childhood friend who spent Saturdays playing with his kids at full volume, in nothing but a cape and dun-ta-duns. As I mentioned earlier, that led to Blanket Warrior, one of my kids' favorite games. In Blanket Warrior, I put a blanket over my head and become a kung fu master. Any kid who gets close to me gets sucked into the blanket, "beat up" (i.e., tickled), and spit out. Meanwhile, the rest of the kids are trying to take down the Blanket Warrior. The only way for them to win is to stop me, and since they can't stop me, the game keeps going until someone gets hurt and starts crying. It can't be me, though, even though I get punched and kicked ferociously. Uriah in particular is a machine. He's like the T-1000 in *The Terminator*. He just keeps coming at me. It's scary, actually.

We also love Nerf battles. I never lose at those because I'm a "camper," as my kids call me. I won't give up; I'll hide in a closet for an hour straight, sweat beads running down my face, until someone walks in front of me. Then—*pow!*—I take them out.

It's funny how the older two boys, especially, want affection, but they look for that affection in the form of being chased, caught, and tickled. Anaya loves to play games, but she is good with any sort of attention. She'll play Barbies with me or help me assemble a table; as long as we're together, she's happy. Uziah, too, craves attention, and he usually gets it by climbing all over me while I'm trying to do something else. He's probably the most insatiable of them all.

I love it. I don't *always* love it, because playing and spending time on their level is exhausting and sometimes painful, especially as I get older. I have literally begun stretching more because things are starting to hurt that didn't used to hurt, and I want to continue being a dad who chases them around and shows them love the way they best receive it—through time spent together.

BECOME LIKE A CHILD

Jesus said, "Unless you change and become like little children, you will never enter the kingdom of heaven" (Matthew 18:3). While he was talking about spiritual things, I think the same thing could be said for developing a deeper relationship with your kids. You've got to meet them on their terms, where they are at, speaking the language they understand. Often, that's the language of play. You have to become childish again.

YOU'VE GOT TO MEET THEM ON THEIR TERMS, WHERE THEY ARE AT, SPEAKING THE LANGUAGE THEY UNDERSTAND.

I'm using *childish* on purpose because the word is often given a negative connotation by adults, as if being childish were wrong. But by definition, children are childish—and that's okay. They are willing to be dramatic and throw themselves wholeheartedly into games. They imagine, pretend, yell, and laugh. They are fully present, and they don't even care what they might look like to others, because they're lost in the joy of the moment. Their childishness is fun to watch, and it's contagious.

As fathers, entering *their* world through play is a better way to connect with them than expecting them to always meet us in our mature world. That means becoming more like them, at least for a few minutes. Obviously, even in your play, you still have to be the adult in the room. You can't throw a temper tantrum when you get hit in the crotch during Blanket Warrior; you just take it like a man. However, you do reconnect with your "inner child," and those minutes of childish play with your kids will be the highlight of their day—and probably yours.

Why is it hard to play with our kids sometimes? I think there are several reasons. First, we might not have learned to do it. This is why access is so important: When we see other people relating to their kids in ways we didn't experience ourselves, we catch a vision for what is possible. Growing up, I didn't really play with my father. With the exception of Mr. Hale, I don't recall any of my friends having fathers who played with them much either. Often, as in my case, their fathers simply weren't in the home. Letting myself play is something I've learned by doing it with my kids, and I owe that learning to the time and space I've had with them as a stay-at-home dad. They have taught me to be childish again.

Second, it can be hard to play with our kids because—let's be honest—sometimes we just don't want to do it. Our family recently moved to a very small, very warm house, and roughhousing with a herd of sweaty children isn't exactly a hygienic experience. Sometimes I have to say, "First put on deodorant, and then we'll play." Other times, we might have work to do, and getting interrupted by play and then trying to return to our work can be challenging.

Finally, society often seems to look down on men having fun. Somewhere around high school or college, many of us became convinced that play is for kids and work is for adults. While guys playing sports as a hobby is allowed by our culture (at least to a point), those who play video games, build Lego sets, or enjoy other nonproductive activities are often looked at as a little weird, as if they never really grew up. And yet research has frequently con-firmed the benefits of play for adults, not just children.

Regarding this last point, our own desire and need to play can be a connection point with our kids. My daughter loves to play video games with me, for example. Fortunately, my wife fully understands the value of those times. Instead of giving me a to-do list when she sees us on the couch playing games and yelling at the screen, she values those times, knowing I'm investing in our daughter.

Of course, I'm also not up at random hours of the night playing *Call of Duty* with my bros. If you do that, I'm not condemning you—I play tennis regularly, and I'm not here to judge how you use your free time. But if your leisure time has to be limited anywhere, I suggest prioritizing play with your kids over playing with other people. Pickup basketball games with your buddies or hobbies like fantasy football can be awesome, but if you're experiencing too much demand on your time, try to think of ways your built-in need for fun and relaxation could be merged with your kids' desire to play *with you*.

I hope my heart is coming through here. I'm not trying to limit you or guilt trip you in any way but rather to awaken the idea that if you let yourself meet your kids where they are at, in their world, there are probably games and activities you will enjoy together.

Give yourself permission to enjoy those moments with them. Be willing to look ridiculous, to get down on the ground, to laugh until you cry, or to pull a muscle or two. We are all still children in God's eyes, and we need to be okay with being children in our own eyes too.

WHY PLAYING WITH YOUR KIDS MATTERS

The most obvious and immediate benefit of playing with your kids is having fun. That's all that matters to them, and they aren't thinking any more deeply than that. But as fathers, it can be helpful to realize that we're accomplishing a lot more than just having fun when we set our work down and make time to play with our children. In other words, play *is* productive, and it deserves a spot on our to-do lists. Let's look at a few of the benefits.

1. YOU REINFORCE YOUR KIDS' BELIEF THAT YOU ENJOY AND LOVE THEM.

Put yourself in their shoes for a minute. A good chunk of their day is given over to being told what to do, what to learn, and how they need to change. That's normal because they're growing by massive amounts each day. But if all they ever hear from us as their parents is what they need to *fix*, they might start thinking we love a future version of them—that they need to change something before they can be accepted. Likewise, if all they ever hear is what they need to *do*, they might think we value them for their contribution and productivity, not for who they are as individuals.

Play unmasks both of those lies. When we play with our kids, we tell them we enjoy them now, just as they are, and we tell them we love them for who they are, not for what they can produce. They need that. They'll spend the rest of their lives fighting the same culture we do, a culture that shouts that we are not enough and productivity is all that matters. They need an inner voice that counteracts those things by reminding them they are valuable, loved, and worthy just as they are.

2. YOU STRENGTHEN YOUR BOND WITH YOUR KIDS.

Playing together causes both you and your kids to release the hormone oxytocin, also known as the love hormone, which increases bonding. You are literally wired to play with your children, and playtime builds an emotional and relational connection with your kids that works both ways.

This is dope if you're a goal-oriented kind of person, because if you want to build long-term relationships with your kids—which I think we all do as fathers—you can put "play with them" on your schedule. Viewing play that way can help you justify setting aside the urgent but eternal workload or the never-ending social engagements. Play shouldn't be last on the priority list. It's not optional, and it's not a waste of time. Play is an investment in your bond with your kids that will last longer and be remembered more fondly than whether you met that minor but urgent deadline or had lunch with that friend who asks for advice but never takes it.

As fathers, playing with our kids is one of our superpowers. Sometimes dads get a little jealous or feel left out because mothers have such a close, nurturing connection with their kids. Dads can nurture and hug too, of course, but many of us tend to be even better at playing with them. I don't know if it's an innate part of being male or if it's a result of culture and stereotypes, but it seems like we naturally tend to throw our kids in the air, tickle them, chase them, play ball with them, go exploring with them, and in general *do* things with them rather than just *be* with them. It's worth noting that oxytocin is the same hormone released when moms breastfeed or when parents cuddle with their children. So rather than feeling left out, strengthen your bond by doing what you do best: Play with them.

Nothing is stronger than family, and playtime is a form of intimacy and connection that builds the family as a unit. Play reminds us that we don't only clean the house together, eat together, or work together, but we also just love hanging out and being in the same room. Shared positive experiences are bonding, and what is more positive than laughing together around the kitchen table until you can hardly breathe?

3. YOU SHOW YOUR KIDS THAT THEY ARE THE MOST IMPORTANT PART OF YOUR LIFE.

Years ago, I bought a used table on Facebook Marketplace for a hundred dollars. It was a long table with a leaf in it, four chairs, and a bench that went on one side. I snatched that deal up, and I was so proud of it. Over the years, the table got all scratched up and messed up, but since it cost only a hundred bucks, it didn't matter.

Once we started making videos, though, we kept having to show our dining room table on sponsored videos. In that context, the table was a little embarrassing. So we finally moved it to the backyard and bought a brand-new $1,300 table, plus chairs.

We had it for barely a week before Anaya used a Sharpie on the table. We tried to get the stain off, but we ended up messing up some of the finish. I remember sighing, looking at my wife, and saying, "You know, we just have to recognize that this is where we are in life. We are not supposed to have nice things."

The truth is, we could train our children not to mess up our nice things. But by doing so we would be showing them that we value our purchases more than their experiments in art and creativity.

On occasion we go visit a family member of ours who has chosen to protect her furniture. She won't even let kids sit on it. When her grandkids visit, they sit on the floor. Her stuff is thirty years old, so I guess you could say her plan worked . . . but why? What's the point? And what's the cost?

I don't want to live a life that teaches my kids that their messiness is a problem to me, because life itself is messy. Being a kid is messy. Being a father is messy. Families are messy.

When you play with your kids, you reassure them that they are more important than your schedule, your work, your friends, or anything else. I'm not saying those things aren't important, but they are not *as* important. Taking time to simply enjoy your kids proves to them that your love is real and tangible. They don't just hear it; they see it and feel it.

4. YOU CHANGE YOURSELF.

Play is for our kids, but it's for us too. Whether it's jumping on a trampoline, playing with Barbies, or competing in hockey, play transforms us as well as our children.

How? First, it reminds us that the people who are most important to us love and need us just as we are. In a world that criticizes and judges us all the time, that's a healthy thing to keep in mind. I'm the worst at remembering this. I get in my own head way too often, then I start stressing, calculating, strategizing, and prioritizing, all in an effort to prove something to my inner critic.

My kids don't even think in those terms, though, and I'm sure yours don't either. We don't have to meet sales goals or earn titles to impress them—we just need to see them and be with them. Play helps us remember that the people who matter most already have our admiration.

Second, play reminds us not to take ourselves too seriously. Again, I tend to overestimate my own importance, which is not a healthy way to think. I've found that play is a great antidote to self-importance because rolling around on the floor with somebody's armpit in my face is anything but dignified.

There's a story in the Bible where King David danced in praise to God while in his underclothes. It wasn't quite dun-ta-duns, but it was close. His wife got on his case because she thought he made a fool of himself in public. He replied, "It was before the LORD, who chose me . . . I will celebrate before the LORD. I will become even more undignified than this" (2 Samuel 6:21–22). We need a similar attitude when we're playing with our kids; we are doing this for them, not for anyone else, and we'd take ourselves even less seriously and be more undignified if it meant meeting more of their needs.

Third, I'm convinced play helps heal childhood wounds. I'm not a psychologist, but I've seen how a healthy relationship with my kids is restoring areas of pain, lack, and trauma in my own life. It's not just play, either, but hugs, time, words of affection, and more, all working together to rewrite my family experience. If you grew up with a lack of parental attention or with abuse, I believe playing with your kids is one way to bring a degree of healing to those areas. Their unconditional acceptance is therapeutic. Their innocence is restorative. Their joy is contagious. Let your childhood wounds be healed by becoming childish again.

BLACK BOY JOY, BLACK GIRL MAGIC

When I was a little boy, I used to love waving at police cars. I remember clearly when the police stopped waving back though. I was eight years old. *Eight.* When I was seven, they would wave to me, but then I started looking a little older, and suddenly they just stared at me. I had become suspicious. I was now a potential threat. Can you imagine how that felt to a kid?

Now, as a father, I have to teach my kids about the police. I don't tell them the police are evil, but I tell them that police and other authority figures will often perceive them as threats simply because of the color of their skin, and that can be very dangerous. When Theo cut his hair, one of my biggest concerns was—and is—that he looks so much older. He's a young man, not just a cute little kid, and that can scare some people. It's the sad reality of living in America today.

How are we going to change that? Legislation and marches are important, but for me, one of the primary strategies is simply normalizing Black joy. I want a suspicious world to keep seeing happy Black families until they change their internal narrative. I want it to be just as normal and accepted and expected for Black kids to play and laugh as it is for white kids, and I want Black kids to be seen as naturally innocent, just as other kids are.

"Black boy joy" is a phrase I use a lot, and its counterpart is "Black girl magic." For me, Black boy joy and Black girl magic are about Black kids having fun without anyone judging them or rejecting them. Those phrases are about letting our kids be fully themselves, uninhibited and unreserved, without fear or shame.

Sometimes I'll get a little "correction" from people when I use language like this. People (usually white people) will say, "You mean boy joy" or "You mean girl magic," as if the word *Black* triggers them somehow. I use the full terms intentionally though. I'm trying to push back against a society that often has a tough time with Black people having fun. I can't speak for other countries, but in the US, the concept of a Black family being healthy, united, and loving doesn't historically fit with the stereotypes we see on TV.

Playing with my kids and posting it on social media is, in one sense, an act of defiance. It's a way to take a stand against a world that wants to rob us of our humanity and lock us into preconceived ideas of what we can and can't do. It's also a rallying cry because I want other families to show their joy to the world too.

Joy doesn't belong to one group or one race. It's a universal trait. That's why kids all over the world play without inhibitions. Only as we grow older do we internalize the pain and prejudices that divide us. Play is a way of tearing down walls, abolishing the things that separate us, and proclaiming that we are all equal as humans who were made in the image of God.

We can't let the pressures, tragedies, or abuses that are built into a racialized culture control the narrative. I say this as a Black person, but I know other marginalized groups have similar experiences. Our joy is an act of rebellion that will change the world, one family at a time. That's how we rewrite the narrative, and it's how we take our power back.

Black boy joy and Black girl magic will transform society, and as a father, I can empower my kids by investing in their well-being and joy. If that means playing with them, I'll play with them. If it means creating a safe space for them to laugh and love, I'll create a safe space. If it means giving people access so we can be proof of a happy Black family, then I'll give access.

Whether you are Black or not, don't let anyone tell you how you can or can't enjoy your family. Instead, follow your internal mission and honor the people closest to it. Who cares what people think? Let your joy shine. Put on capes and run around the neighborhood, or go on bike rides, or make up games, or create new traditions. It's your family, and they need your joy.

08

Chapter Number

THE GIFT OF PRESENCE

Title

Start

When Theo, my oldest child, was still a baby, I worked for a company that managed equipment at Camp Pendleton, a Marine base north of San Diego. Every day the infantry unit would turn in the equipment they had checked out, and I'd have to receive it and process it for cleaning. It was always covered in all kinds of crap: dirt, twigs, sweat, mud, and who knows what else. By the end of the day, I was also dirty and covered in crap. When I got home, I couldn't kiss Theo and cuddle with him like I wanted to because the stuff clinging to me would have gotten all over him. So I'd take my clothes off just inside the door and head straight to the shower. Once I was clean I could spend time with him in a hygienic way.

That image of getting rid of the grime that clung to me has stuck with me, because as fathers, we've got to do the same thing on an internal level. Fathering ourselves means dealing with the stuff that's contaminating our thoughts and emotions so we can engage with our kids in healthy ways. When we get home from work or when outside pressure is too high, we need to take a moment to clean off the dirt from the day and set aside everything that's not important or helpful, because it can prevent us from being present at home.

That's hard to do sometimes. It's one thing to be able to see the dirt that sticks to your clothes and realize you need a shower before you can hug your kids. But it's another to recognize the inner stuff that sticks to your soul and your emotions: the worries, the fear, the trauma, the distractions. And yet it's even more important to wash those things off before they get on your kids.

How we respond to the pressure and craziness of the world outside our homes can deeply affect our children and our families. If we walk into the house with negative energy, we can sabotage the atmosphere. Instead of elevating it, we undermine it. Similarly, if we come home distracted and withdrawn, we won't be the active, engaged dads our kids need. We'll be there physically but not mentally or emotionally.

As I've mentioned, when I was growing up my dad lived in California while I lived in Baltimore. I knew he was always a call away—but I still didn't call. He'd say he was always available, but there was something about not being physically present that made it difficult for me to connect with him. If he were in the other room, I think it would have been a lot easier. When we did hang out in the summer, certain moments—such as going to get haircuts together—were so valuable to me, more than he might have realized.

In retrospect, what I wanted was his full, undivided, tangible attention. My kids want the same thing, and I'm sure yours do too. They need us to be with them in body, soul, mind, and spirit. They need our time and energy, our mental focus, and our emotional availability.

Attention is the most valuable currency we have as human beings. That's why brands pay me to post about their products; with all the competing voices out there, it's hard to get people to pay attention and watch something. When we show up for our kids and engage wholeheartedly, when we're available and attentive, we truly are gifts to our families. Our gift is our attentive presence, not just our paycheck or our problem-solving abilities, and making the effort to be present is a crucial part of the work we do as fathers.

quote

ATTENTION IS THE MOST VALUABLE CURRENCY WE HAVE AS HUMAN BEINGS.

Our attention is a limited resource, and it's easy to get distracted. My children have a lot of access to me because I'm home most of the time. Often I'll be in the middle of editing a video, and I'll feel a body next to me. Other times I'll wake up in the morning and see a silhouette of a child just standing there with crazy hair, not talking, just waiting for me to wake up. It's frightening. But just because I am in the vicinity doesn't mean they feel invited into my space. It doesn't mean I'm mentally or emotionally available to them. When they're trying to play with me, talk with me, or just be with me, what they're asking for is my *undivided attention*. That's what being present means: not being distracted by anything, whether internal or external, so I can be fully engaged with them in the moment.

As fathers, our attention is incredibly valuable to our kids. It tells them they matter—not just to us but in the universe. Our focus and attention give them security, peace, and self-worth. When we are fully present and attentive, we strengthen the family unit and create connections that will extend throughout their lives.

PRESENCE IS GOOD WORK

Being present means staying focused, making yourself available, and bringing your best self to your family. I'm not going to lie:

That's exhausting at times. It's challenging work, but it's good work. It's the kind of work we must do in order to be the fathers our kids need and deserve.

On a practical level, how can you do the good work of being present? Let's break it down into four key components.

1. LOOK IN THE MIRROR: SELF-AWARENESS

A big part of self-awareness is noticing what is going on inside your mind and emotions. Rather than always looking outward and trying to fix or change the world around you, begin by looking inward. Is there anything within you that you need to be aware of to become a better father?

This goes back to the idea of noticing what "sticks" to you. What does stress do to you, and how does it come out in your tone or actions? How about anxiety or depression? Anger? Financial pressure? Insecurity over your shortcomings? Frustration with a client or coworker? You can't beat yourself up over the fact that you have negative thoughts and feelings swirling in your head, because you're human, and you're carrying a lot. But you also don't have to let those things steal from your time with your kids.

Along with becoming more aware of your thoughts and feelings, self-awareness means noticing how you fill your time and what activities you choose to engage in. If you're going to give your full, undivided attention to your kids, it's important to recognize things that might be distracting you from quality time with family. As I said in the last chapter, I'm not here to judge you for how you use your free time, and I think it's healthy to have hobbies and do things you enjoy. Just make sure they are not too much of a distraction from the attention your kids need from you. This usually isn't a matter of right and wrong but rather a matter of degrees. How *much* of your focus is on other things? How *much* time and energy do they get, and what is left for your family?

Often the things we do to distract ourselves are not about trying to avoid our kids at all but rather about avoiding ourselves. Maybe we are frustrated, ashamed, angry, insecure, anxious, depressed, or otherwise wounded and in need of healing. Our distractions might be about filling a void we should be dealing with in a different way. I don't mean to get too deep and analytical here, but it's worth asking ourselves, "Why do I need to play this sport? Hang out with this person? Spend this much time scrolling my phone? Watch this much TV? Drink this much alcohol? Eat this much junk food?" If we're engaging in things that distract us from giving our kids the attention they need because we're trying to hide something God wants to heal, we need to find a better way.

2. CHOOSE WHAT YOU FOCUS ON: SELF-CONTROL

After we identify whatever is keeping us from being fully present, we need to move from self-awareness to *self-control*. It's one thing to recognize we're stressed-out; it's another to choose to let that pressure go, take a deep breath, and be fully present for our kids. That's why we sit in the driveway for five minutes if we need to, until the adrenaline dissipates and we can walk into the house with a smile and energy. It's why we deal with traumas from our own past so we can be the best versions of ourselves for our kids.

Self-control is one of our greatest assets as fathers because it empowers us to choose our responses to the pressures and chaos we face. There is freedom in exercising self-control. It gives us our autonomy back. We don't have to be swept away by the rushing currents of stress, anger, or fear that so often swirl around us all day long. We can do the hard but healthy work of regulating our emotions and channeling our thoughts out of dark spirals of doom and into a better place.

3. TIMING IS EVERYTHING: DELAYED GRATIFICATION

One of the challenges of being present for our kids is that our homes are supposed to be places for *us* to decompress and rejuvenate too. After a long day, it's natural to pull into the driveway with a longing for some space and peace. In the evening, after working all day, I want silence, I want gumbo, I want reruns of *The Office*, and I want nobody to be on the toilet in case I need to use it.

Fatherhood is a lot bigger (and better) than what would make us feel relaxed and comfortable though. Often we can't cater only to our needs because we've got kids who have been waiting for us to come home like cute but ravenous vultures. So after a day of work, we have to be mentally and emotionally prepared for round two: to keep giving, loving, and listening to our kids. There will be time for self-care and gumbo, but it will usually be *after* we meet the family's immediate needs. We're the adults in the home, after all, which means we know (at least in theory) how to postpone our desire for relaxation and pleasure until the right moment. That's called delayed gratification. Kids are absolutely terrible at waiting to get their needs met, but as fathers, it's a fact of life.

The good news is that the act of loving your kids and letting yourself be loved by them is even better than gumbo. It's rejuvenating in itself. When I let my kids climb all over me, when I let myself relax and laugh and stop being guarded, their love actually brings healing to the craziness of the day. Then, when they finally go to bed, I can get the peace and silence I crave. (Except they rarely stay in bed, so I have to keep putting them back down, one after the other, like that Whac-A-Mole game where you molly-wop creepy little moles in the head but they never actually stay down.)

4. SET HEALTHY BOUNDARIES: PRESENCE OVER PROBLEM-SOLVING

If you've been gone all day, it's almost guaranteed you'll have some stuff to do when you get home. That's why it's important to separate the value of what you do for the family from the value of your presence. You might need to set some boundaries on what you can and can't do when you first walk in the door in order to protect your time with your kids.

A couple of years ago, there was a three-week period in which every single day, I was informed the moment I got home that the toilet was clogged again. My first activity upon arrival was to go plunge poop out of the toilet, and it just ruined my mood. After the first week, I started getting frustrated. I bought different kinds of plungers and snakes, but of course I didn't really know how to use them, so my insecurities and feelings of inadequacy aggravated me even more. It got to the point where I hardly wanted to come home because I knew our toilet from hell would be waiting for me. Finally I called a handyman, and he fished a Beyblade out of the toilet. I was like, "Who put a Beyblade down the toilet?" And one of my children, who shall remain unnamed, confessed, "I did, but I didn't want to tell you." Welcome to fatherhood.

In retrospect, I could have handled the whole thing differently. To start with, I should have called a handyman sooner, but of course I didn't know that. What I *could* have done, though, was tell my wife, "I don't even want to know about the toilet until after I've spent time with the kids. Give me an hour, then tell me about it." That's how I should have protected my presence, how I should have allowed myself to be welcomed. Enjoying my family first would have been better than showing up to "Yo, toilet, my man."

Notice that setting this kind of limit is different from plopping down in front of a football game with a drink in my hand the moment I get home, all in the name of self-care. It's tough on my wife to be with the kids all day, so the first thing I should do is relieve her of that pressure and be the father my kids need in those moments. If she gives me a task before that, though, or if I give myself a task, I'll be distracted. So this isn't just about self-care; it's about prioritizing your presence. It's self-care with a purpose because you're making sure you can give the best of yourself to your family—and the "best" is your attention and availability, not your plumbing prowess.

YOU NEED THIS TOO

We need to realize how important connection and intimacy are for us men—not just for our kids. I think a lot of men long for intimacy their entire lives, but they don't even know they need it. One of the greatest gifts of fatherhood and family is this connection, this belonging, which family provides. We've got to see it for what it's worth though.

When our first son was born, I looked forward to teaching him a lot of things: how to crawl, how to walk, how to talk, how to play, how to read. But for the first few months of their existence, babies can't do any of that. They only eat, sleep, and poop. So for most of the day, as long as you've met those three needs, you just hold them. It forces you to slow down, to be quiet, to build a connection that goes beyond just *doing*. It's a beautiful thing.

This quiet, steady intimacy is something you must protect as they grow older, because life quickly gets crazier. As your responsibilities grow, it's easy to feel so pulled and pushed by the demands of the fatherhood role that you forget the value of being present, not just for them but for you.

One time I told my therapist that I often don't feel like part of my own family. I'm there for everyone else, but I don't always let myself be a member of the family. I'm too busy herding kids from one thing to the next, or calling plumbers, or catching lizards that sneaked into the house, or working to put food on the table. The tyranny of the urgent takes over.

That feeling of not belonging is a red flag, and I know it. I also know it's more in my head than anything else, because my kids and wife really do love me unconditionally. However, it can *feel* like I'm primarily appreciated for what I contribute because we have four kids and a dog, so I will never be caught up with the things that need to be done, and there will always be demands on my time. Instead of being ruled by the tyranny of that reality, at times I need to deliberately set aside what still must be done, slow my pace, take off some pressure, be part of the family, and let myself be loved for who I am—not just what I do.

To be honest, I struggle with this. I think it's probably a challenge for many fathers. We've got to do and be so much for so many people, and yet we also have needs: to connect, to belong, to be loved, to feel valued, to feel safe.

I told my wife a while back that nobody really hugs me. I hug everyone else, but I don't have anyone who does it for me. So she made me put my arms down and let her hug me. Surprisingly, it was a lot harder than I would have thought. I don't know if I'm naturally wired to be the protector and provider or if it's what I've learned over time, but it felt vulnerable to let myself be hugged—vulnerable, but also necessary.

It's crazy that I would struggle with letting myself be hugged when I have no problem understanding how much my *kids* need to be hugged. I love hugs, but I don't remember being hugged much growing up, except by my sister. She lived in California with our dad, so we saw each other only in the summer. Yet again, I can hear my therapist telling me to show myself the same grace and compassion I show my kids. Hugging and cuddling my kids is one of the most beautiful parts of fatherhood for me. Of course, it's one thing when my five-year-old comes over and squeezes me, and it's another when it's my eleven-year-old. At that age, there are so many prerequisites. Did he shower and put on deodorant? Why does his breath stink? Why does he need a hug now, when it's hot and we're both sweaty? It's the most inopportune time. Plus, he's a big kid now, so there's a level of strength I need to endure this. I stop myself from saying those things—usually—because I understand he just needs affection.

I love their hugs. I'll cuddle with them until they're eighteen, if they let me and if they shower regularly. I think it's supposed to be that way, because as fathers we are the safe place our kids are meant to go to. If we don't hug them, the streets will. Somebody else will. And those people and places might not have the best intentions.

Did you catch the contradiction in all that? On one hand, I

sometimes feel like I'm not hugged by anyone; on the other, my kids would hug me all day long if I let them. I've learned two things. First, I need to let people like my wife and my good friends embrace me and make me feel loved and safe. I need to be held, and I don't have to be the hero all the time. And second, I need to father myself into accepting that not only is this my family, but also I'm a key part of it—and I'm loved and valued for more than what I do. It's my presence they need and love most, not my performance, my perfection, my paycheck, or my plumbing services.

Bottom line: By choosing to set aside to-do lists and simply be present, we are meeting our kids' need for connection as well as our own. That's good work.

quote

AS FATHERS WE ARE THE SAFE PLACE OUR KIDS ARE MEANT TO GO TO.

ACCEPT ALL THE INVITATIONS YOU CAN

Your kids will often invite you to interact with them. These invitations might be direct: "Dad, come play with us!" Other times, they are more subtle. They drop hints, or they climb all over you and get in your face, or they act moody. They can't necessarily put into words what they want, but if you're paying attention, you'll realize they're looking for your undivided attention. If you can say yes to the invitation, the value and worth they receive is priceless.

Now, let's be real, they are always going to want more of our time than we can give them, especially when they are young. We *want* to be with them, but we also have jobs. We have spouses. We have social commitments. We have back pain. We have houses that always need work, cars that break down at the worst times, taxes to file, doctor appointments to drive to, friends we want to spend time with, and so much more.

Plus, sometimes we're just tired, or what they want to do sounds boring. We won't always want to play with our kids, listen to their stories, or watch their shows with them. Sometimes we'll be in the middle of something and it's not a good time, or we're tired or stressed-out. Sometimes we're on the clock or have a project due in two hours. Sometimes it's bedtime and we know they're just looking for an excuse to stay up.

At times, one of my kids will start a sentence and I'm like, *Oh, my gosh, I do not care, and can you say it faster?* I don't tell them that, but I'm thinking it, and I have to remind myself that efficiency matters a lot less than their self-esteem. If I interrupt them or shut them down, what does that say to them about their voice and their value? I want them to have confidence in their own voice, which means I can't interrupt them out of irritation. I want their inner voice to tell them, "When I speak, people listen." Many people don't speak up for themselves, and I think some of them learned that because no one listened to them as children.

We get to choose whether to accept the invitation or put it off until later. There's no shame in this choice, but there is a cost. When you choose to accept or reject an invitation, make sure you consider that cost.

First, you will often be called to sacrifice time, comfort, or productivity. You could lose an hour of work time, scratch up your knees, or miss some sleep. You might lose concentration or momentum on something, or you might not get through your to-do list. Sometimes I'll be on an editing roll, and I'm focused. I'm killing the edit. But then a child comes in and says, "Hey, can you wipe my butt?" or "Dad, I need help putting this Lego set together." That's all it takes sometimes to totally derail my progress. That's part of the work of fatherhood though: recognizing I will need to work extra hard to get back in the zone later, but it will be worth it.

The work of fatherhood is also dealing with the emotional toll that comes from being constantly available, because always being present and attentive to your children is exhausting. Before my kids were born, I didn't know I could get emotionally tired. It's not that my mind is tired, but my emotions get frazzled and depleted. I'll be worn out from hearing crying, complaining, and noise in general, and I'll feel as if I don't have any more cares for whatever is happening right then. But somehow I have to muster up the energy.

One time my daughter was sick, and I documented on video how many times I got up that night. She had breathing issues, so first I had to rub her back to help her settle down. Then she threw up. Then she had a coughing fit. Then she had to go pee. I just kept documenting: "Okay, it's one in the morning and this happened . . . Now it's three o'clock and I'm doing this . . . Now it's four, and I'm scared to go back to sleep because I gotta get up in two hours." People without kids who watched the video were appalled, but parents felt seen. We've all learned that being present as a parent is work sometimes. It's worth it, but it's work.

On the other hand, there is a bigger cost to refusing the invitation. The obvious cost is the missed opportunities to connect with them (which, as I've said, is sometimes inevitable). If we say no too often, though, the cost gets higher. Every time we respond to them, we are training them to see us and approach us a certain way because they're always learning. We build a set of expectations in their heads, and we create a narrative about ourselves and our relationship with them. They might learn we are busy, hardworking, responsible fathers—but not fun or present fathers. Plus, they may start to assume *they* are the problem; if they were more mature, more interesting, or maybe more like us, then we'd want to be with them. Those are not the narratives we want to build, and they aren't even accurate—but that's what kids can pick up when their fathers refuse too many of their invitations to connect.

Put yourself in your kids' place. Asking for our attention and time can be a vulnerable thing for them to do, especially as they get older. Rejection by anyone hurts, and rejection by their father is especially tough. Even if they're not wounded by it, they often don't have the resilience or attention span to keep asking and pushing. They'll find other ways to meet their needs for connection.

I've noticed that when I say, "I'll play later," it often doesn't happen. I've had situations where I've put one of my kids off for a while, then when I finish my task and finally say, "All right, I'm ready to play now," they reply, "I don't wanna play anymore." Then I have to pursue them. Because I said "later" instead of responding when they wanted my attention, I'm now working from a deficit.

I've never regretted being present, and I haven't missed out on anything in life by being a better dad. I've never put my phone down and gotten involved, then looked back later and said, "That was a waste of time." I don't think anyone on their deathbed says, "I wish I would have gotten more work done." Usually as people get older, their regret is that they didn't invest more in their family, because family matters more than anything.

Again, this isn't about shame or about putting an impossible burden on ourselves. It's about recognizing that our kids' need for our presence and attention is a real need, not just a whim or a luxury. We can say no if we want to or need to, but if it happens too much, we're subtly training our kids to find another place for that type of affection or outlet.

The key is to accept as many invitations *as you can*. Don't set the bar too high for yourself, but don't set it too low either. You might even need to create rules for yourself: "I'm going to roughhouse with them three times a week" or something like that. The idea is to build a sustainable relationship with them so you can be present as much as possible, even if it means cutting into a few other responsibilities, because you understand how valuable your presence and attention are.

You can also invite your kids to be involved in what you're doing. If you run an errand, take someone with you. If you're fixing something, let them help, even though their help is probably going to slow you down. If you're watching TV, cuddle with them or scratch their back. If you're cooking dinner, bring them into the kitchen with you. Take the initiative to pull your kids into your routine instead of expecting them to force themselves into it.

Another option if your kids want to play is to negotiate a little. "I'll build a fort with you in the living room, but go clean your room first because I don't want a mess in there and a mess in here. That way, when it's time to go to bed, you won't have to pick up your toys." You're not trying to avoid playing with them, but you're establishing boundaries and habits that make play sustainable.

If you do have to say no, take the time to explain yourself. "Dad really wants to play right now, but I've got to do this thing right now because it's important. I love you so much though, and you're important to me, so we'll do something together as soon as I finish this." Just taking the time to explain that to a kid, even though they're only four or five, can help frame your "rejection" in a way that builds them up rather than discourages them.

The good news is your kids will give you many, many invitations. Even if you haven't been as involved and present as you know you should be, it's not too late. Even if you were in a bad mood yesterday and snapped at a child who got on your nerves, today is a new day. Even if you grew up with a distracted or distant father, you can still learn new habits and embrace new possibilities.

Being present is a learned skill, and you'll get better with repetition. You won't be perfect at this, but try it anyway. Do it wrong until you learn to do it right. If you blow it now and again, apologize. The amazing thing about kids is they are so forgiving, so full of grace. They'll give you another chance because they want and need your presence so much.

The real power here is found not in being perfectly present but in being *consistently* present. Presence over the long term makes the difference. If your normal habit is to accept as many invitations as you can, when you do have to say no, it probably won't affect them because you've built up such a deposit of trust and connection over time.

We're going to mess up sometimes, and life is too crazy to expect perfection—but we can be present. We are here for our kids, and that's not going to change. Even on tough days, we're going to be here for them, giving them our full attention, showing up for them the best we can, and valuing those moments when we connect and engage. Our gift is our presence, and it's something we can give them every single day.

ADVENTURE

Start

If you have kids, you already know how unpredictable fatherhood can be. Every day is an adventure, which is a beautiful thing.

As fathers, it's important to choose to view the craziness that way—as a source of beauty—rather than resenting it or wishing the chaos would all go away. If you are overly focused on control or efficiency, or if you let fear write the narrative in your head, you risk missing out on much of the experience. After all, the best moments as a family are usually unplanned.

Fatherhood is more than a role to fill or a duty to carry out; it's an adventure, and it deserves to be lived to the fullest. In **chapter 9, "Tornadoes, Trampolines, and the Art of Adventure,"** we talk about embracing the unexpected and living free from fear.

Embracing the unexpected means letting go of the need to control or predict everything, and that can be a challenge at times. In **chapter 10, "Fatherhood on the Fly,"** we look at why things like perfection, control, and balance are overrated, and we explore how to adjust and adapt to anything life throws our way.

Chapter Number

TORNADOES, TRAMPOLINES, AND THE ART OF ADVENTURE

Title

— Start

A few years ago, we rented an RV and took an epic (and maybe overly ambitious) cross-country road trip with our kids. We started in California; went through Arizona, Texas, Louisiana, and a few other states; and ended up in North Carolina. The experience was . . . a lot. Mostly it was awesome because we saw so many family members and friends along the way and built great memories. There were definitely a few emotional meltdowns along the way though—mine as well as the kids'. Packing six loud people into one tiny RV is asking for drama. Add in black water tank woes, bug infestations, and sweltering heat, and you've got a recipe for all kinds of crazy. But it was worth it—so much so that we recently decided to buy an RV so the crazy can continue.

I think the most memorable moment of that trip was a tornado scare when we were visiting cousins in Dallas. The electricity was out, the wind was blowing, and the sky was insane. I had never seen clouds like that before, and I was genuinely scared. I was running between the house and the RV, trying to get the vehicle tightened down in case a twister came too close. At one point, we were looking out the back window of the house, and a neighbor's trampoline flew over the fence and just kept going. I don't mean a little Jazzercise trampoline either. This was a Costco-sized trampoline, and it sailed through the air like a plastic bag on a summer breeze.

I was racing around with terror in my voice, imagining all the things that could go wrong. Meanwhile, my wife was laughing. *Laughing.* Somehow she was enjoying the adrenaline of the moment. My kids thought it was fun too, and Uriah was even pleading with me to let him go outside. Honestly, what is wrong with my family? I have it all on video because even if my life is ending within the next fifteen minutes, I'm not going to pass up the opportunity to get some great footage.

Thankfully, the tornado warning turned out to be nothing but wind and rain. The next day was sunny and clear, and the kids spent the morning playing with their cousins. I don't know if the neighbors ever found their trampoline, but beyond a few fallen branches, there was no sign of the storm from the day before. As it turned out, the stress and fear were unnecessary because all my worst-case scenarios never came to pass.

As I look back on that road trip—not just the tornado scare but other incidents along the way—I can clearly see two things: first, the sheer joy of going on adventures together as a family; and second, the potential for fear to undermine those family experiences. In Dallas, erring on the side of caution was wise because I've seen enough documentaries and news reports to know you don't mess with Mother Nature. However, in situations that aren't quite so life-and-death, I want to make sure I'm not so focused on "the side of caution" that I miss out on living life fully with my family.

As fathers, we need to embrace and even seek out adventure with our families; at the same time, we need to navigate the uncertainty, unpredictability, and stress that often accompany adventure. It's not necessarily wrong to think of the bad things that could happen and prepare for them, but if those bad things are consuming our minds, twisting our emotions, and showing up in our reactions, we need to be careful. When the storms (literal and figurative) blow over, we want positive memories to be left behind, not just stories of how dad freaked out. If we're going to err at all in this back-and-forth between adventure and caution, let's err on the side of experiencing our family to the fullest. In other words, let's be willing to become adventurous.

ERR ON THE SIDE OF ADVENTURE

When I was a traveling musician, I would get terrible stage fright. That might seem contradictory considering my career choice, but despite my public persona, I really don't like being the center of attention. I had what I now realize is imposter syndrome, so I felt like I wasn't a "real" musician, and I'd imagine the worst before every performance. Eventually I got tired of building up all that negative anticipation—the dread I felt of something going terribly wrong—and started trying to enjoy each show. Once I discovered the freedom in that mindset, I remember wishing I could go back in time and experience certain events without the paralyzing fear I felt as they were happening.

I've gotten better with practice, but I still deal with this. When I face new scenarios or things I'm not confident I can handle, I tend to worry first and relax later. I have to make an intentional effort to look past what could go wrong and see what could go right. I have to therapize myself and father myself. Otherwise, my overactive imagination runs away with me, and I start visualizing what the media outlets are going to report when my entire family gets sucked into a tornado like something out of *The Wizard of Oz*.

I'll hold full-on conversations in my head between therapist Glen and nervous Glen:

"Dude, what are you anxious about?"

"I think something will go wrong."

"Have things gone wrong in the past?"

"Well, rarely."

"Okay, so normally things don't go wrong. Why do you think something bad will happen today?"

"I don't know. I'm just scared, okay?"

"Okay. Now, when something does go wrong, what do you usually do?"

"Well, I figure it out. I find a solution."

"And is today any different? Won't you just figure it out?"

"Yeah, I guess so."

"Okay. Now, what's the *best* thing that could happen?"

"Well, my kids could have fun, we could get closer as a family . . ."

It's a whole process. I need to talk myself into a healthy place, or my inner bully can ruin the party. The process is work, but it's liberating work. I'd much rather do this in my own mind than let it spill out all over my kids and wife through my words and actions.

What's crazy is that most of the things I worry about never come to pass—like that tornado. Then, once things are calm again, I usually realize I've gotten myself all worked up over an illusion, a ghost that never materialized. It's a waste of energy, and this tendency can distance me from my family rather than help me be more present.

Embracing adventure is not just a personality thing. It's not as though fearful fathers are on one end of some spectrum while adventurous fathers are on another. I think all of us crave fun and exciting moments with our kids, but unchecked fear can sneak in and sabotage our capacity to enjoy the crazy road trip of life. We need to deal with the inner voices that whisper, "Things will go wrong" or "You're going to fail," so the natural desire to enjoy our families can shine through.

quote →

FATHER YOURSELF THROUGH THE INNER OBSTACLES UNTIL YOU DISCOVER THE FREEDOM GOD PUT WITHIN YOU.

I'm not telling you to just "be more adventurous." This isn't the chapter where I try to convince you to buy an RV or move to a farm. That's what we did, but that's not right for most people. Instead, I'm simply inviting you to pay attention to the way you show up in this road trip called life. I'm asking you to do the same thing I have to do: Father yourself through the inner obstacles until you discover the freedom God put within you, a freedom to enjoy even the crazy moments because they are part of the journey too. Adventure is built into fatherhood, and with a little bit of intentionality, it can become one of the main drivers for lifelong family memories.

HOW TO EMBRACE ADVENTURE

Adventure looks different for everyone, and its definition changes from season to season. Don't put pressure on yourself to look like another family, especially if you only see them on social media. You can't compare your daily routine to someone else's highlight reel. What you and your family call *adventure* will depend on your personalities, abilities, likes and dislikes, season of life, and resources, and that's more than okay—it's the whole point. You are building *your* family, not some culture-driven idea of what the perfect family is or does.

More than a specific list of things you "should" do as a family, make sure you approach adventure as a *value* and a *mindset*. As a value, adventure is something you're willing to invest in; as a mindset, it's something you're always alert to discover. In that spirit, let me give you a few specific principles my wife and I try to follow with our family.

1. CREATE ADVENTURE OPPORTUNITIES.

Our Realtor, a guy named Mark, used to own an incredible RV, a Jayco Seneca, that was perfect: diesel engine, bunkhouse, the works. I was so envious when I saw it. After only two or three years, though, he sold it. I was shocked, so I asked him what happened.

"My boys wouldn't go on trips with me anymore," he said. "My seventeen-year-old doesn't like to go, and my fifteen-year-old won't go if his brother doesn't. So I didn't need it anymore."

My oldest was ten at the time, and that conversation was a wakeup call for me. If we were going to get an RV, we needed to do it soon, before they grew up. There would be only so many opportunities to go on family vacations. Right now, my kids love to be with me. They climb all over me before I even wake up, sticking things in my ears and begging to play. They'll go with me on errands or hang out with me while I'm doing things around the house. But the day will come when their schedules and priorities change, and they might not want to be with me as much. We've got to make the most of the time we have now, which means being intentional about building memories as a family.

"Creating opportunities" doesn't have to be as complicated as buying an RV. It simply means building a life that purposefully includes adventure. Sometimes that might be a trip or event you budget for and organize, but often, adventure is more of a philosophy and a lifestyle. If you are intentional about adventure, you're paying attention to the present moment with curiosity and a willingness to try things, explore, and take risks.

For us, moving out of the city to a farm was meant to accomplish that. We wanted to put ourselves in a new environment where we'd have different experiences because we knew it would make us grow as a family. So now, instead of moving my car once a week so street sweepers can get by, I'm catching snakes, chasing off coyotes, and dealing with a mouse family that took up residence in the leather seats of our car. My kids are seeing the world from a different angle, a new perspective, and they're better because of it.

What if, instead of orienting our lives around comfort, getting ahead, or buying stuff, we prioritized experiences and making memories? My wife is amazing at this. She'll have the most out-of-the-box ideas for activities, but they often work way better than I would have imagined. Her willingness to do spontaneous things without worrying about whether they will "fail" is inspiring to me.

Failure is a matter of perspective anyway. If you are a very goal-oriented or destination-oriented person, you might need to rethink how you approach family activities. Even if a hike, a trip, or a purchase doesn't turn out the way you expected it to, that doesn't necessarily make it a failure. If memories were made and fun was had, the activity or trip was a success. Sure, you might decide never to try that particular thing again, or you might make some changes next time around—but if adventure itself was the goal, you succeeded.

2. OVERCOME THE BARRIERS TO ENTRY.

Life is full, and it's easy to take the path of least resistance. Rather than looking for adventure or attempting new things, we can be tempted to just protect and perfect what we have. That mentality tends to squash adventure though. It values routine, it seeks comfort, and it plays things safe to a fault.

If you want to embrace a more adventurous family experience, sometimes you have to force yourself to do stuff that isn't comfortable, easy, cheap, or fun—but it's good for your family, and *it's what you really do want to do*. Think about that for a moment. We *want* adventure, we want bonding, we want memories. We want to see new places and experience new things together. We want our kids to learn to get along. We want to set an example of courage and curiosity. These are all good, desirable goals.

Maybe we don't love the hassle and stress that go into making those things happen, but the results are worth it. As fathers, when we put in the time, energy, and money to create memorable experiences with our families, we generally don't look back afterward, after it's all over, and call it a waste. Usually we say, "We should do things like this more often!"

That's what I mean by things we really want to do. If we want the rewards of adventure, we'll have to overcome the barriers to entry:

- Adventure takes time.
- Adventure costs money.
- Adventure includes risk or uncertainty.
- Adventure requires planning and initiative.
- Adventure is tiring and sometimes exhausting.
- Adventure stretches your brain, budget, and body.

It's a lot easier to sit on the couch and watch television every Saturday and Sunday, but is that creating the kind of memories you want? Is that building the kind of kids you want? The path of least resistance is usually also the path to the least potential for reward.

There's no shame in watching TV, of course. You can't take a road trip every weekend, and a secure, stable home life will also build security and memories. This isn't about forcing yourself to do more than you should do but rather about recognizing that our human tendency is usually to make the least possible effort—and then regret not doing more.

As I described above, *fear* is one of the things that can sabotage adventure—but there are others. A *desire for comfort* can do the same thing. For me, comfort is my kryptonite. I know myself well, and I can easily let my preference for peace, quiet, and ease get in the way of getting out there and doing things with my kids. My kids don't need a complacent dad though; they need an involved one, which means I usually end up tired and sore. We need to make sure we aren't saying no to certain ideas or opportunities just because they are a pain in the butt.

Busyness is another potential obstacle. Sometimes we fill our lives up with so many activities, commitments, and obligations that we have no margin left for the unexpected. We will always have more to do than we have time to do it, though, so we'll have to make choices along the way. We might need to schedule our adventures rather than leaving them to chance.

Here's another obstacle to adventure: *hyperefficiency.* Adventures are rarely "efficient" or "productive," at least by the metrics of our culture. Going on bike rides with your kids takes time. Spending a day or two at an amusement park costs money.

Often, you'll have to switch off the side of your brain that wants to drive, produce, and control so you can be fully present. In general, I'm always trying to accomplish a mission, my wife is trying to stop and smell the roses, and my kids are trying to have their own experiences and go on their own missions. None of that is wrong. Sometimes we need to set aside our own preferences or preconceived ideas of what "should" happen and simply go with the flow.

Finally, *lack of resources* can be a real barrier to entry. Don't go bankrupt chasing adrenaline, but don't let money tell you how you can parent either. All kinds of adventures are free or cheap: Go for a walk, ride bikes together, visit a museum, or play Frisbee at the park. The same goes for other resources you might be lacking. If you're short on time, what can you do as a family that is close by and will take only an afternoon? If you're lacking energy, how could you guard some of your strength during the day so you have some left for your family? If you need mental space, what stressors could you eliminate so your kids have your full attention?

When we look at these obstacles as temporary barriers that stand in the way of what we genuinely want to do rather than reasons to give up, we begin to think differently. We are creative, intelligent, strong people with years' worth of experience solving problems and pursuing goals. If we use those skills and qualities to attack obstacles that keep us from family adventure, we can usually find ways to make things work.

3. FOCUS ON THE JOURNEY.

A friend of mine told me his family of five once took a vacation they called their "follow the dart" trip. They rented a minivan and packed for a ten-day road trip, all without knowing where they would go. Then they threw a dart at a map of the western half of the United States. They were hoping for Yellowstone or the Grand Canyon, but instead, the dart landed on a random backwater town in the middle of the Eastern Oregon desert.

They drove there anyway. The only rule was that if anyone wanted to stop and see something, they would do it. There was no itinerary, no urgency, no pressure. It took them two leisurely days to get to the town because they visited family members and a couple of parks along the way. After looking around (which didn't take long), they threw another dart at a map and kept going. Over ten days, they drove three thousand miles and saw volcanic lava beds, a ghost town, Las Vegas, the California coast, theme parks, and more, all without a plan.

My friend told me that when his wife first suggested the idea, he thought it was terrible, a disaster in the making. But to this day, it's one of their favorite vacations ever. I told him we're going to steal the idea, but we'll probably use a bow and arrow instead of a dart.

You've likely heard some variation of the saying "It's not about the destination; it's about the journey." As a goal-driven person, I hate to admit this, but there's a lot of truth to that phrase. When we make family times too much about getting somewhere or doing something, it can be difficult to enjoy the present because we see happiness as something waiting for us in the future, once we "arrive." The journey becomes a necessary evil, something to tolerate before the real fun begins. That's a waste of a good journey though.

Now, destinations do matter. If we're on a literal road trip and urgently need to empty the black water tank, you'd better believe I'm going to be focused on our destination. That's only part of the experience, though, which is what I try to remind myself. With anything we're doing as a family, whether a trip or just an activity nearby, I've learned to intentionally slow down, be present, and enjoy what is happening now.

If we hurry too much, we tend to miss the beauty along the way. We did one road trip to the Grand Canyon, and we left at three a.m. and arrived at seven a.m. We made great time—but I don't have any stories from that part of the trip. The drive was productive but less memorable. Plus, I felt distanced from the family, like I was just a chauffeur providing a service. On top of that, Anaya ended up getting sick and spending the next night in the hospital, so I was absolutely beat. In retrospect, it would have been better to go a little slower and be involved as a family rather than killing myself just to save an hour of driving.

In general, it's best to go at the pace of your family. Again, this is true not just for road trips but for any adventure or activity. Be part of the family yourself, and let their excitement, curiosity, and speed (or lack thereof!) guide you.

I think the mix of togetherness, flexibility, and convenience is what excites us about an RV, because cramming our family into a van for long trips is painful. We've done it, but it involves a lot of drama and so many potty breaks. Anaya has the world's smallest bladder, and she has to stop every hour. Meanwhile one kid will be hungry, another will be carsick, and Uzi will be trying to break out of his car seat. It's a lot. In an RV, the kids can snack, play, or pee as needed, and I don't have to pull over at every rest stop and watch sadly as all the semitrucks I just passed get in front of us again.

Literal road trips are only a subset of adventure, so don't think

quote

IT'S BEST TO GO AT THE PACE OF YOUR FAMILY.

I'm trying to turn you into a road warrior if you'd rather spend a week at a beach resort. It's not where you go, what you do there, or what mode of transportation you prefer but rather the mindset you adopt: one that decides to enjoy the entire experience, starting now.

4. IMAGINE MORE POSSIBILITIES THAN PROBLEMS.

I'm sure by now you've realized I am highly skilled at imagining all the things that could go wrong in any scenario. It's my spiritual gift. My brain is quick to feed me a list of negative outcomes, and then my emotions get on board too. While wisdom and caution are good things, negativity can get out of hand quickly.

The best way I've found to counteract this isn't to shut down my analytical brain but rather to get it to include a few positive outcomes in its hyperactive analysis. By default, our brains often fixate on danger. It's a survival instinct. But we don't have to live in that place, and we definitely don't have to parent from that place. Instead, we can use our God-given creativity and reasoning skills to imagine the good things that could happen if we step out of our comfort zones and pursue growth and adventure. This is true not just for family adventures but for any change or decision.

When you feel your mind starting to wander down the what-if trail, guide it in a positive direction.

- What if this move to a different city builds up our marriage?
- What if this trip turns out better than we even expect?
- What if this new school helps our kids discover their future careers?
- What if our kids remember this vacation for the rest of their lives?

- What if this career change is an opportunity for me to grow and build a better future for my family?
- What if these people we just met or the neighbors who just moved in end up becoming amazing friends?
- What if this family activity teaches me more about my kids or myself?

Do you see what these questions do? They turn you away from fear and toward adventure. Your mind is your most powerful tool to experience life, and if you learn to use it right, it will change the way you show up in any situation. The ramifications of this truth for your family life are huge. You can't predict or control all the things your family is going to face, but you can choose to be a person of faith and positivity. You can train your mind to see things through a positive lens, discovering adventure and fun even in moments of chaos or ambiguity.

Is finding snakes on our property terrifying, or is it an adventure? Is being miles from the nearest restaurant inconvenient, or is it a blessing? Is homeschooling our children hard work, or is it an enriching, empowering experience for us? *All* those things are true. The ones we choose to focus on the most will determine our experience though.

I know how I would have handled moving to a tiny house on a remote farm in the middle of a hot summer in the past, and I'm actually proud of how I've changed. With this move, I've been able to keep my expectations high, and it's made the experience so much more enjoyable. We've faced some unexpected things along the way, like water so yellow we couldn't bathe in it, a heat wave that one poor mini-split and multiple fans couldn't remedy, a biblical-level plague of ants in the kitchen, and the previously mentioned rodent takeover of our vehicle. But because I'm choosing every day—sometimes every hour—to embrace adventure, I'm more attuned to the good things that happen and more resilient to the bad ones. I wish I would have learned this attitude as a kid, but at least I'm learning it now, and my kids are too.

Take a moment and visualize your next family adventure. What will it be? What are the exciting things that might happen? Does anything in your heart or mind need to change so you can embrace that adventure? What's the next step you should take to get the ball rolling?

If you can do these four things—create more opportunities for adventure, overcome barriers to entry, focus on the journey, and train your brain to see possibilities—you're going to have more fun as a family. Yes, things will go wrong once in a while, but they'll do that whether you are embracing adventure or not. It's far better to go into those moments with a positive mindset.

As you embrace adventure as a family, you'll find ways to enjoy even the craziest moments. You're a responsible adult, so when a tornado sends massive lawn furniture flying across the yard in front of you, you'll plan an escape route or find the safest place in the house to hunker down just in case—but you will *also* find beauty and bonding in the adventures you share. In the small moments and the big ones, you'll show your kids the joys of curiosity, exploration, and discovery.

Chapter Number

FATHERHOOD ON THE FLY

Title

Start

've been a hip-hop artist for many years, and I'm a part of the culture. It's not just the beats and rhymes that move me but the creativity and authenticity that hip-hop represents. Those two things were built into the genre from the very beginning.

In case you're not familiar with the origins of hip-hop, it all started in 1973 in the South Bronx section of New York City. A Jamaican artist who went by the name DJ Kool Herc noticed that crowds loved to dance to the instrumental breaks in funk and soul records. He started setting up two turntables with the same record, then he'd mix and loop the breaks in real time so people could dance longer. His block parties became famous, and other DJs started imitating his "breakbeat" technique. And so hip-hop was born.

Back then, DJs usually had a hype man called an emcee (which comes from MC, or master of ceremonies) who would make up rhymes on the spot to keep the energy up and get the crowd involved. The emcee was an assistant, a backup to the DJ, who would help him set things up and in return get a few minutes on the mic while the DJ was mixing the beat. Often emcees would spit lines about real-life scenarios: what was happening in the streets right then, people who had passed away, police brutality, and more. Over the years, these emcees, or rappers, became stars in their own right; but at the beginning, they worked with DJs to create live experiences that were unplanned, raw, and high-energy.

To me, hip-hop is a lot like fatherhood. The difference is that you're the DJ and the emcee at the same time. You're making stuff up on the fly, teaching truths, and keeping the energy high while spinning discs and solving problems in the background. It's controlled chaos, and it's fly. You've got to be creative and spontaneous because you never know what's going to happen, but you're there for it.

Fatherhood is messy—there's no denying that—but the mess comes with creativity. As fathers, we need to be able to see the beauty that's being birthed from the messiness. We should "feel" the vibe of our family and work with it, roll with it, and run with it to create something new. We talked about embracing adventure in the last chapter, and embracing messiness is the other side of the same coin. You rarely build memories without at least a degree of chaos and craziness.

As a dad, you're not a drill sergeant demanding perfect lines and doling out push-ups when people fail. Instead, you're an artist. You're a hype man, a performer, an innovator, a creative. You carry out your role live, and you're responding to an ever-changing environment and an "audience" that can't decide if they want pancakes or cereal for breakfast.

The creative potential this role provides is mind-boggling. You are facilitating the development of mini humans. Of course the experience is a little bizarre at times, a little unpredictable, but would you have it any other way? The point isn't to control all the variables but rather to learn how to respond in real time to whatever the moment demands. It's fatherhood on the fly: pivoting, improvising, and adjusting as you go.

If we're going to successfully embrace the messiness of fatherhood and family, I believe there are several illusions we need to stop chasing. These myths seem as though they'd be helpful, but they are actually impossible to obtain. If we go after them too hard, we risk undermining the very things that make family so beautiful. The way I see it, we need to let go of

- our desire for **perfection**,
- our pursuit of **balance**, and
- our tendency to **control**.

Perfection, balance, and control are helpful concepts, but they make terrible goals. Yes, we try to get better at things, but perfection just ain't gonna happen. Similarly, we strive to have a safe, secure home environment, but it's never going to be perfectly stable and balanced because kids are constantly changing. And while getting stuff done (i.e., control) is necessary, the ultimate goal is to build our children on the inside, not regulate them from the outside. Like an emcee on the mic, we're tasked with innovation, not perfection; with movement, not balance; and with inspiration, not control.

I find myself struggling to let go of these three myths on a regular basis, and I suspect you might as well. Parenting is a constant back-and-forth tension between improving, stabilizing, and directing the madness on one hand without stifling their creativity or suffocating their joy on the other. Let's take a few moments to explore why we should release these three illusions and embrace the mess a little more.

quote

WE'RE TASKED WITH INNOVATION, NOT PERFECTION; WITH MOVEMENT, NOT BALANCE; AND WITH INSPIRATION, NOT CONTROL.

THE MYTH OF PERFECTION: THEY'LL
GET SAND IN THEIR CREVICES

My wife loves the beach. When we lived closer to the ocean, she wanted to go all the time, every day if possible, with all the kids. I would groan every time because when we'd get home, sand would be everywhere. It was so frustrating. Sand would be in the car, on their clothes, in their hair, under their fingernails, and wedged in every crack and crevice of their bodies.

At the same time, I know the chaos was always worth it. Yvette has helped teach me how to embrace the craziness without getting too overwhelmed by it. She does the best job of making great memories and taking photos. She grew up as a middle child, and she doesn't have a lot of pictures of herself from her childhood—so she's determined that won't be the story for any of our kids. The sand will fall out of their crevices eventually (probably just before we go back to the beach), but the fun times are going to stick in their minds and hearts. That matters a lot more than perfect hygiene or a clean car.

Perfection is overrated, and it's an impossible goal anyway. And yet so many of us think we need to have a perfect family. It's been ingrained in us that our kids' behavior is a direct reflection of our parenting, which is—to put it politely—crap. They're going to make mistakes because they're still learning how to be alive. We can't let that embarrass us or condemn us.

As fathers, I think sometimes we want our kids to be like commercials for the experience of our family, so we try to get them to be perfect representations of who we are. But we're not even perfect ourselves, so why would we pressure our kids to perfectly represent us? All that does is create feelings of inadequacy and trauma. They might grow up assuming they're not good enough simply because they were less than perfect, which would be a sad outcome indeed.

In parenting, perfection is a myth that needs to be debunked. That's the reason I don't clean up our house before I shoot a video. It's why Yvette and I often upload content that highlights our mistakes and what we learned through them rather than showcasing our successes. It's why we disagree with each other on our podcast. We don't have a perfect family, and we're not trying to have one. We're trying to have a healthy family, a happy family, a loving family, a fun family, a learning family, and a united family—but not a perfect one. As a matter of fact, a stubborn pursuit of perfection would undermine everything else on that list.

One time I took my kids back to Baltimore, and we went to see my old elementary school. In front of the school was a huge tree, and because it was fall, giant piles of leaves were on the ground. My kids had never seen that before. They started running and jumping into the leaves. They were loving every minute of it, and so were Yvette and I. Then I noticed a family member who was with us. She looked a little grossed out, and she said in a critical tone, "They seem very . . . free."

She didn't mean it as a compliment, but I took it as one. I want my kids to be able to express their "wild child" side. I want them to be free. To me, a free child is one who is confident, who takes risks, who can speak their mind, and who can identify their emotions. They probably have scraped knees and jacked up elbows, and they might have a couple of scars, but it's because they're not afraid of making mistakes and learning along the way.

Freedom, messiness, and learning go together. That's why demanding perfection from our kids is so damaging. It can short-circuit the trial-and-error process that is built into childhood (and adulthood, actually). Instead of valuing perfection, we need to teach our kids how to ask questions, try new things, and learn along the way.

When I was assembling our trampoline recently, a family member called, and I told her what I was doing. Her first comment was, "Oh, be careful! Those things are dangerous. The kids are going to fall."

I know she was just being cautious, but the comment kind of got under my skin. If my first and loudest thought is *They're going to fall*, I'm not giving my kids any hope or freedom. If I protect them from every possible mistake or suffering, it means I'm not allowing them to experience life, which will actually harm them.

Yes, they're going to fall, and they're going to hurt themselves. But the ultimate goal of childhood is not to avoid getting hurt, and the purpose of life is not simply to avoid death. We were created to love life, to live it fully, and to pursue our full potential.

Obviously we're talking about things within normal parameters here. It's not like my five-year-old is skydiving. My kids are going to the beach, playing in leaf piles, and jumping on trampolines. Sure, letting the wild child come out will mean sticks in their hair, sand in their crevices, scrapes on their knees, and holes in their clothes, but it also means they feel safe and free enough to love life and learn as they go. That beats perfection any day.

THE MYTH OF BALANCE: LEARN THE ART OF JUGGLING

Besides letting go of a desire for perfection, we also need to let go of our need for balance. By *balance* I mean the idea that we can get everything situated and coordinated, then step back and admire our handiwork as if nothing will ever need to change. When we use this term, we often assume we can find a perfect arrangement of our many responsibilities so nothing gets too much attention, nothing gets too little, and everything works in perfect synchrony.

The reality is much more fluid and unpredictable than that. We have work pressures, house repairs, financial obligations, health needs, social commitments, and so much more. Add to that the everchanging and usually urgent needs of our kids, and it's no wonder our days rarely go as planned.

This ongoing movement is why balance is not a good long-term goal. We might get everything working for a day, a week, or a month, but sooner or later, things are going to change. Stuff will slip and shift, and we'll have to balance it all over again.

Think about a circus performer on a unicycle, juggling three balls with one hand while spinning plates on his nose and carrying an umbrella in the other hand. He has to fight gravity *and* keep things moving. His success—and his life—depend on making sure nothing shifts unexpectedly. That might work with balls, plates, and umbrellas, but kids don't sit still. There's a reason circus performers don't carry four small children in their arms.

The last time we had family photos taken, I set up a video camera too. The difference between the final photo and the video is hilarious. In the photo we all looked the same direction, all smiled, all stayed stationary. In the video, though, we seemed to be herding cats for two straight hours. Which one was more accurate—the video or the photo? The video, of course. The photo is a snapshot of one miraculous moment, but it's not reality. In the same way, our day-to-day lives are going to be in constant motion, not perfect stability or balance.

I think a better word than *balance* is *juggling*. In juggling you focus specifically on each ball, one at a time. It's dynamic and interactive, just like hip-hop. Balls are literally falling around you, but you don't panic because falling is part of the pattern. You catch them and throw them back in the air, then you turn your attention to the next ball. Instead of trying to fight gravity, you work with it. Instead of trying to get everything as stationary as possible, you make the movement the point.

To be honest, I often feel overwhelmed as a parent. I regularly find myself having to choose between finishing a video edit, running an errand I've put off for a week already, playing with a child who is hanging off my head, spending time with my wife, cooking, cleaning, or going for a walk for my mental and physical health. The reality is that they are *all* important. If I try to balance the things that tug on me, I'll just end up frustrated because there are way too many things to hold at once. But if I juggle them by focusing on each one in turn, I'll have a lot more success. A vital part of the art of fatherhood is learning how to attend to the million things that demand your attention *in the right way and at the right moment* so nothing important falls to the ground.

Notice I said "important." Not every ball you throw in the air is worth catching. When your goal is balance, you tend to add more and more responsibilities and activities into your schedule; but when you stop balancing and start juggling—pouring your time and energy into each thing in turn—you learn how valuable those things are, and you're forced to let go of the demands that don't deserve your focus.

I've come to realize that some of the things that steal my time and attention are connected to other people's expectations. Those are balls I'd rather drop if it means I keep more important ones in the air. For example, years ago, my wife tended to overcommit to social engagements. One time she informed me, "We're going to a birthday party for so-and-so's kid."

It was a workday, and it was in the middle of the day, so I said, "No, I have to work. I'm not going."

"But they're going to think you don't care about their kid."

"Well, I do care. But even if they think I don't, that doesn't change anything because I still have to go to work."

Another time, also years ago, a couple in our church got married. Yvette told them, "I'm so happy for you. As a wedding gift, Glen is going to DJ your wedding."

I was so mad. I didn't even like DJing. It was just something I was doing at the time to bring in extra cash. I told her, "You're a math teacher, but I'd never volunteer you to tutor someone else's kid."

"What, you don't care about my friends?" she said. "These are my people."

It turned into a full-on argument. We worked through it, though, and we figured out where the boundaries needed to be. Today, Yvette protects my time, and I protect hers. We both know we can keep only so many balls in the air at once, and we have to be careful what we give our time and attention to.

For me, the metaphor of juggling is about being fully present for each thing. Rather than spreading your time and attention out over everything—which usually results in feelings of shame, because no matter what you do, you're not doing something else—you give yourself completely to what is in front of you. If you're playing with your kids, let them have your full attention. If you're going on a date with your wife, make her the focus of your time together. If you're getting your work done, do that wholeheartedly, without feeling guilty for focusing on it.

There's a verse in the Bible that says, "Whatever your hand finds to do, do it with all your might" (Ecclesiastes 9:10). I see a parallel to the idea of juggling. Do what is in front of you to the best of your ability, then do the next thing, then the next thing. If you keep that up, you'll find that most of the balls—the important ones, at least—will be just fine while they're sailing through the air. This is more sustainable and less schizophrenic than tight-roping along while carrying everything at once.

THE MYTH OF CONTROL: THE MESS IS YOUR MASTERPIECE

Control, as I've said before, is an illusion. We're never fully in control, and even if we get close, all it takes is one random bad thing to happen and we realize how powerless human beings are. We can't control the weather, the economy, traffic, pandemics, our genes, the flow of time, natural disasters, or the other humans who inhabit our spaces.

My wife and I often joke that we have a fifth child, a ghost, who does all the stuff nobody confesses to. In reality, the fifth child is the combination and culmination of the entire family. Things just happen. Stuff breaks. When they're all together, there's an emergence, a product, that is bigger than the individual family members, and it's beyond our control.

I try to stay in control though. I really do. Sometimes I'll find unflushed turds in the toilet, which makes me mad because flushing the toilet seems like a basic part of civilized existence. So I'll investigate. If I follow the clues, I can figure out who it was. If there's no toilet paper in the toilet, it means someone didn't wipe their butt. I know for sure that I have three kids who wipe their butts. So that leaves Uzi. Plus, his diet is basically chicken, oatmeal, and hot dogs, so his poop always looks the same. If he's clearly the culprit, I'll say, "Uzi, did you flush the toilet?" And he'll say, "Yeah, I flushed." Nothing I can say will convince him he didn't flush. It must be the ghost, the fifth child, who left those turds.

Crazy, out-of-pocket stuff just happens. We have a kid who sleepwalks, for example. I traumatized him the first time it happened because he was peeing on the cabinets. I yelled, "Hey! What are you doing?" He woke up and freaked out.

Yvette said, "Babe, you scared him. He was sleeping."

"Well, what was I supposed to say? He was peeing on the cabinet with the clean towels in it. There was pee everywhere."

I learned that when he sleepwalks, I have to be gentle. I have to say, "Hey, buddy. Wake up. You're not in the bathroom. You're in the wrong place." I need to help him figure out where he is. Even if he's currently hosing down the towels, it's more important to care for him than to control him.

When you're single, you can almost convince yourself you're in control. You set your schedule, pick your clothes, choose your social engagements, create your budget. You can't control all the variables, but you can get close enough to think absolute order is attainable if you just try a little harder.

Then you get married. Instantly, maintaining the illusion becomes more difficult because someone else is sharing your space. They're a grown adult, though, and you love each other and try to work together, so you can still get close to control.

And then the first baby comes along, and the illusion of control disappears as quickly as a full night's sleep. It's immediately obvious that this baby is not going to operate on your timetable, bow to your expectations, or bend to your will. They can't even understand you, much less obey you. So you learn to adapt to their needs.

As they get older, they learn basic human skills, which you might think means they can be trained into orderliness. But you quickly discover that along with their newfound skills, they have something called free will . . . and now you're screwed. The older they get, the *less* you can control them.

That's a good thing. You're raising humans, not puppets, pets, robots, or clones. Their free will is messy, but the mess is meant to be shaped and formed, not eliminated. Remember, you're working together with God to create masterpieces, works of art who should learn from you without being controlled by you, particularly as they get older and develop more independence.

Now, I'm not saying they are totally *out* of your control either. It's just that they are not fully under *your* control. Ultimately, you are teaching them something far better, which is *self*-control. As dads, we sometimes think the solution to their bad behavior and crazy decisions is to make them bend to our will. While we should expect obedience when we establish rules, our end game cannot be controlling them but rather serving and protecting them so they can grow into the self-confident, self-directed, self-actualized people God wants them to be.

It's easy to see the mess, but sometimes it's harder to see the masterpiece that is emerging. That's where, as fathers, we have to make sure we're focusing not just on the noise level or the number of toys on the floor but on who our children are growing up to be.

A lot of the things that get on our nerves right now won't matter in five years. The reactions we have and the words we say *will* matter though. Those things get ingrained in our children's minds and hearts. They become their inner voice—a voice that tells them either they are not enough or that they are just who they need to be.

These three myths—perfection, balance, and control—aren't doing us any favors as fathers. The sooner we can replace them with more realistic, healthy mindsets, the more we'll enjoy our role as dads and the better we'll be at fatherhood. Instead of *perfection*, let's focus on learning and growth. Instead of *balance*, let's prioritize presence and giving our full attention to whatever we're doing. And instead of *controlling* our kids, let's guide and empower them as they mature.

THEIR FREE WILL IS MESSY, BUT THE MESS IS MEANT TO BE SHAPED AND FORMED, NOT ELIMINATED.

Fatherhood is a live experience, not a recorded performance. It takes place in real time, and you don't get the luxury of planning, perfecting, and polishing everything. That's okay, because the best experiences often happen when you go with the flow, letting yourself be real and present and free in the moment. Just like hip-hop.

06

Part Number

FAMILY

Title

Start

You are more than just a father bringing home a paycheck or changing diapers, and your kids are more than just small humans in your home. You're a family. That is bigger than any one role or person. Together, you are building something new, a family unit that is specifically yours.

Each family is different, and that's beautiful. Your goal is not to force everyone or anyone in your home to fit a mold but rather to help create something new: a family that has not existed before and is unique in the world.

Chapter 11, "Your Family's Song," is about seeing your family as a whole and creating a safe place for each family member to be their authentic, full self. Each member has a part to play, and together you create a beautiful harmony.

Beyond the immediate family, we need to be part of a larger community. This is the topic of chapter 12, "These Are My People," which explores our need to have other men and families in our lives to mutually strengthen and encourage each other.

Chapter Number

YOUR FAMILY'S SONG

Title

Start

Do you have a favorite song? If so, think about why it means so much to you. Is it the lyrics, the beat, the instruments? All of the above? Or maybe it's the feelings it evokes or a memory or relationship it's connected to. For whatever reason, that song sticks in your head and your heart.

For me, one of my favorite songs I've written is called "The Greeting." Unlike many songs, it came together quickly and easily. I had little to do with the creation of the sounds, and I wrote the lyrics in about twenty minutes. While I love that song, I've found that a lot of people prefer one called "I Got the Juice," which I collaborated on with the group the Dream Junkies. That track demanded a lot of effort from an entire team of people.

I could go down the list of every song I've had the privilege of working on, and each one has its own story, its own characteristics, its own appeal. Not everyone will like them all, and that's okay. No song will be everybody's favorite because songs don't work that way, and neither do humans. Songs are supposed to be unique. They resonate with people in unpredictable ways, which is why everyone's music choices are so personal, so colorful, so interesting.

Like songs, families are unique. We all have our own "sound," our own harmony, and that's the way it's meant to be. If my family is your favorite, feel free to ask yourself why. Maybe it's possible to manifest things you believe about my family in your own. All of us "do family" our own way, and that's a beautiful thing.

Just as a song is the product of different instruments and voices that come together as one, so families are the result of the individual members who make them up. The unique makeup of your family, the "sound" you project to the world, is a blend of the people in your home. Each member brings their unique personality, temperament, values, goals, and quirks into the mix, and the track they mix is beautiful. It's your song, your gift to the world, and you should be proud of it.

ALL OF US "DO FAMILY" OUR OWN WAY, AND THAT'S A BEAUTIFUL THING.

Pat's home taught me about this. I'll never forget the way his home sounded—both literally and figuratively. It was loud and chaotic but also warm and encouraging. It buzzed with acceptance, joy, peace, and safety. Walking into his home was like stepping into a harmony. It was a sound I'd never heard before, and I realized right then that this is what a harmonious family feels and sounds like. I could tell by the way the kids spoke to each other, the way Pat and his wife talked, the way everyone seemed to be comfortable in their own skin and made me feel comfortable too. It wasn't clean, and it wasn't quiet at all. The kids were all in earshot, and they were nosy and watching us, listening to us. They felt safe to do that.

When I saw Pat's home, suddenly I was able to imagine myself forming a family and a harmony of my own. Prior to that, I'd mostly seen homes that were anything but harmonious. You've probably been in some of those. You can feel the energy shift when you walk in the room. Things are out of rhythm, instruments are out of tune, and the sounds are grating. They hurt your ears and your heart. You can tell people are putting on a show, that they're trying to be perfect, but the sound is off.

I think a good family makes a beautiful song. If you want to know whether your family has a beautiful song, notice your friends the next time you have company. If you have to ask them to leave because they are so comfortable that they stay late into the night, you probably have a beautiful song. If people come over and just hang out and ask questions, you probably have a beautiful song. If they sit and smile while you interact as a family, you probably have a beautiful song.

When your family has a song, people watch you and learn from you. Even if it's not their favorite sound, they respect what you have. More importantly, your kids feel welcome and safe. They can grow, learn, and thrive because they know they belong, and they see proof that they are valued and appreciated.

Over time, of course, the metaphor breaks down a little because—unlike a song that gets recorded once and then always sounds the same—the sound of your family goes on and on, evolving and flowing into new sounds over the years. With each new family member and in each new season, the music might be a little different; but it's still your family, and it's still your music. Through the craziness of life, and even as your family grows and flows, it should be your favorite song of all.

BETTER TOGETHER

As I've mentioned, my family recently moved into a much smaller house than we were used to. Suddenly we were in each other's faces and spaces all the time—which has required more grace (and deodorant) than ever before. While I'm looking forward to getting a larger place at some point, the closeness has been healthy for us. We can't escape each other, so we've gotten better at being *with* each other. I love that. The proximity forces us to integrate the needs of every individual with the overall good of the family.

Family is about being a unit. I'm not talking about a military unit where everyone looks and acts the same. I'm talking about an organism: something that is alive, changing, and growing, but it works together as one entity with a singular purpose. The value of functioning as a unit is the reason our mission statement for Beleaf in Fatherhood states, "Family is the most important unit on earth. The disconnection of family creates despair. We guide men into father-hood, equipping them to love and lead their family into eternity."

These family units are going to look different from each other, like songs. There might be only one parent in your home, or you might have grandparents living with you as well, or you might be divorced, or you might have kids from multiple marriages, or you might be a father figure to your grandchildren or your nieces and nephews. The point isn't to chase some "ideal" family but to become the family you were meant to be.

When families are healthy, the unit is stronger together than each member would be on their own. In other words, the whole is greater than the sum of its parts. Using the song analogy, a beat by itself is just a beat; lyrics are just poetic phrases; a guitar is just an instrument—but when all those elements come together, when various layers and pieces work as one, a song is created.

In the same way, in the family, something awesome happens when we choose to live, act, and work together. Something new emerges. We not only have each other's backs when someone is weak but we bring out the gifts, talents, and potential in one another that would have remained hidden.

I see this dynamic at play among my kids all the time. Even though they fight and compete sometimes (okay, a lot), it's obvious that each of them is stronger because they have siblings. They learn from each other, rely on each other, and push each other to grow and succeed. They are incredible on their own, but they're even better together.

At the same time, they don't lose their identities. They are wildly different, and the older they get, the more those differences become obvious. Theo is thoughtful, hardworking, athletic, and sharp. Uriah is joyful, spontaneous, affectionate, and compassionate. Anaya is energetic, affectionate, smart as a whip, and strong. Uzi is funny, brave, energetic, and unstoppable. I could list ten more adjectives for each of them. That's not to say the others don't have those qualities but rather that each child has certain strengths and skills in different amounts—and seeing how they are *similar* and *different* at the same time is a beautiful thing.

The same is true for Yvette and me; we bring our uniqueness into the family, and we don't lose that individuality even though we are united as one. She is still Yvette, with all her strengths and talents, and I'm still Glen, with all of mine. We have joined forces, first as a marriage and then as parents, and the combined force is far more effective than it would be if we were separate.

THE ME AND THE WE

As fathers, we must look out for the individual *and* the family. Both of those things matter: the "me" and the "we." Building a family doesn't mean squashing everyone's individuality in the name of unity, but it also doesn't mean throwing a bunch of disconnected humans into a house with no commitment to the common good. This is a foundational truth for any unit of people, but it's especially true for the family unit.

I'm learning the importance of being intentional about both sides of this coin. The easiest side is probably focusing on the family as a unit. It's natural for me to treat them as a collection, especially when we're late and I'm trying to get everyone out the door. I often think of "the kids" as a group or make decisions based on the whole family's needs. That's an important part of being a father, but again, it's only one side of the coin.

The other side requires more intentionality from me: focusing on each child as an individual. I think this is a common occurrence for fathers, especially when our kids are young and our schedules are crazy. We need to keep in mind that each member of the family—no matter how young or old, quiet or loud, mature or immature—is fully a person, created in the image of God, with all the rights that belong to human beings. We can't override one kid's personhood in the name of "what's good for the family."

I've realized that I can't truly know my kids unless I spend time *alone* with each of them. I need quality, one-on-one time to hear what's really in their hearts and understand them fully. Life isn't exactly conducive to that kind of intimacy though. Either we're all rushing around trying to do something or there are too many kids in the room to really have a heart-to-heart convo with anyone. So I have to get creative.

When they were younger, we had a tradition where every night at bedtime, I'd spend the number of minutes with each child that corresponded to their age. So when Theo was eight, he got eight minutes; when Uriah was six, he got six minutes; and so on. I'd read to them, answer questions, cuddle, or whatever they needed. It was good but also exhausting. Plus, it wasn't a sustainable strategy. By the time they grew up and moved out, I was going to be starting bedtime at like five p.m.

Now I make a conscious effort to connect with each child in some way on a regular basis. It helps that we're home a lot, but it still takes intentionality and a good dose of patience to bring someone along on errands or solicit their help with a project. I'm sure this is going to be even *more* important as they grow older, not less important.

Because I care about their individuality, I'm also adamant about not letting them interrupt each other too much. If one child is talking to me, I want to give them my full attention. I think the quieter kids in a family sometimes get talked over and ignored too easily, and they can grow up not valuing their own contributions or opinions.

In a healthy family, every member should contribute with their gifts. Some gifts are definitely going to be louder than others, but they are all important. As fathers, we need to be alert and search for ways to invest in each child, encouraging them and giving them opportunities to bring their full selves to the family. They need to know they matter and that they have something to give the world. What better place to learn that lesson than in the family?

There's a Bible passage that says, "Make me truly happy by agreeing wholeheartedly with each other, loving one another, and working together with one mind and purpose. Don't be selfish; don't try to impress others. Be humble, thinking of others as better than yourselves. Don't look out only for your own interests, but take an interest in others, too" (Philippians 2:2–4 NLT).

That passage describes the mindset I want in my home. I want each of us to look out for our own interests (our rights, needs, dreams, ideas, health, and future) *as well as* the interests of the rest of the family. It's me *and* we; it's your needs *and* our needs. That takes love and mutual commitment, as this passage says, but it's exactly what God designed families to do best.

WHEN ONE SUFFERS

Family is a unique kind of unit because the bond between us runs deep. In most cases, it's in our DNA, our blood, our history. Often we look alike and talk alike. Even as adults we might have our fights and disagreements with our extended family, but if someone is threatened or in need, the family comes together as one.

A few years ago my sister passed away from cancer, which was incredibly painful for me. Right at that time Yvette was going through a difficult time emotionally and mentally. Eventually she realized she needed to take intentional time away to prioritize her well-being, and I carried the parenting load solo for three weeks. Her experience was good work and helpful for her peace of mind; meanwhile I felt abandoned as I grieved alone. We weren't able to stay in close contact during that time, and I was able to see her only once. Even though she left things organized for me, I still found myself overwhelmed a lot. Not only was it hard to handle my work, process my grief, and take care of the family, but I also missed her and was worried about her.

At one point during those weeks, I happened to speak with someone who worked for Eric Thomas, a motivational speaker who has been a big inspiration for me over the years. I had never met Eric personally, but I mentioned to this employee how much a recent message by his boss had encouraged me and how I was struggling to keep my head in a good place. Soon after that, Eric himself called me on FaceTime. The first time he did so, I ignored the call because I didn't recognize the number. He called again, and I thought maybe it was Yvette, stranded somewhere and in need of help, so I answered. I couldn't believe it when he introduced himself as Eric Thomas.

He said, "I heard that you're anxious, that you need encouragement. Let's talk."

I told him what was going on, and he listened to me. Finally he said, "Glen, think about Michael Jordan. The Bulls needed Jordan at 100 percent. They didn't want him to be at 40 percent or 70 percent. They needed him to be fully healthy. Your wife is a star player on your team, so let's get her back to 100 percent. You can handle three weeks. You're going to be fine."

It was a message I needed to hear, not just for my own struggles but also for our family. I remember explaining to my kids that Mom needed some space to rest and focus on herself so she could come back stronger. That could have been just a marriage thing that we kept between us, but it needed to be a family thing. If Mom isn't doing well, it's a family issue, because let's be real: If she ain't good, *we* ain't good.

The lesson I learned was to normalize taking a break to do the deep work necessary to be fully healthy. Not just for her but for my kids and me as well. If Uzi ain't good, we ain't good. If Anaya ain't good, we ain't good. When one member of the family suffers, everyone suffers, and it's everyone's responsibility to step in and help. We're all going to have moments and seasons when we're at 70 percent or even 40 percent. That's when family should really flourish as a place of protection for the member who is weak or suffering until they can get back on their feet.

While Yvette was gone, everyone stepped up to a new level. I remember one day I was supposed to take the kids somewhere, and I was running behind. I had stayed up working late the night before and was having an off day. Theo knew exactly what to do. He made sure the younger kids were dressed, he told everybody to brush their teeth, and he helped me get things back on track. Something in my nature didn't want to lean on my own son or to ask for his help, but I needed him at that moment. Likewise, I need every member of the family. Not just when I'm having an off day but amid the day-in, day-out rhythms of life. I need their gifts, their prayers, their acceptance, their grace.

The Bible compares the faith community to a body when it says, "If one part suffers, every part suffers with it; if one part is honored, every part rejoices with it" (1 Corinthians 12:26). It's the same with the family. What happens to one of us happens to all of us because we are interconnected and interdependent.

> **WHEN ONE MEMBER OF THE FAMILY SUFFERS, EVERYONE SUFFERS, AND IT'S EVERYONE'S RESPONSIBILITY TO STEP IN AND HELP.**

Remember, the family unit exists for its members, not the members for the family. God designed it for the blessing, protection, and empowerment of the people who make it up. It's a tool—a vehicle whose primary purpose is to serve its members, not win awards for the most picture-perfect family.

I get a little nervous when people hold any family up as an ideal to strive for. I hope my family inspires other people, and I'm glad people can learn from us, but at the end of the day, I'm not building a family for them. I'm trying to create the best possible environment for my kids, my wife, and me to thrive in. It's our sound and our song.

When I focus on the needs of each member, I find that the family as a unit usually takes care of itself. Healthy kids and parents will create healthy families, and if we are all at 100 percent, we're going to have a family at 100 percent.

There's a lot of freedom in that truth. Sometimes you might get overwhelmed by the needs of your family, but remember, your family is made up of *people*. You know these people. You love these people. You have history with these people. You probably brought most of these people into this world. (Well, you played a part anyway.) If anyone is qualified to meet their needs, it's you. As you build each of them, and as you work with them to care about not only their own needs but also the needs of the squad, you're going to build a family you're proud of.

It takes work, but it's the good work of fatherhood. To quote Eric Thomas, "You're going to be fine."

AN INVITATION

For a song to really connect to people, it needs to invite people in. The words and music should make people feel welcome and seen. That's what I love about the song I mentioned earlier, "The Greeting." It makes you curious, and it draws you in.

In the same way, when our families are functioning in harmony, people should feel an invitation. As they hear the sound of our family, it will draw them in, make them curious, and help them feel at home.

For me, this aspect of inviting others into my life is very literal because my social media channels give people direct access into our world. For you, it's probably going to look different, and that's fine. Just please remember how valuable you are and that people need to hear your family's song. They are listening and watching, and they need to know what you have discovered about family and fatherhood.

Your family gets to decide the sound you're going to make and the harmony you're going to show to the world. At the end of the day, your family is *your* family. They're *your* people. And they're *your* favorite song.

Your song is not just for you though. It's a song others will hear, and it will change the way they think about family. That's a beautiful thing.

12

Chapter Number

THESE ARE MY PEOPLE

Title

Start

When I first got into a relationship with Yvette, she had a community of people she had grown up with. These people were family to her, like adopted aunts and uncles, which was beautiful.

As I started spending time with this community at Christmas and Thanksgiving, I noticed an interesting dynamic: The women seemed to have a deeper connection than the men, at least from my perspective. After eating together, the women would laugh, play, clean up, and joke around. Meanwhile, most of the men sat in front of the TV and watched football. I'm sure they enjoyed each other's company, but when I imagined my own future, I knew I wanted more camaraderie. I'm not saying their interactions were wrong, but I knew it wasn't enough to sustain me.

Fast-forward a few years, and Yvette and I started getting involved in the small group program at our church. That meant weekly home meetings where we made new friends and began to build community. I saw my wife choosing women to be around her, but I realized I wasn't necessarily choosing their husbands. I wasn't against them, but I wasn't pursuing them either. I had flashbacks to those holiday meals in the early days of our relationship, and I remembered my desire for a deeper connection and community.

So I decided to "choose" the men whose wives were my wife's friends. I liked these guys, and I knew I needed a deep connection with people if I wanted our time together to be as great as the moments my wife shared with her circle. I dreamed of a community of real friends, of men I could be vulnerable and real with, men who would form bonds and be a strength to each other.

This was over a decade ago, when Theo was just born. Over the next few years, our families kept meeting together and building connections, and my wish came true: I felt surrounded by men I could lean on and learn from. We were part of a community I loved.

Life moves fast though. Our group went from having one or two small children between all of us to thirteen, which amped up the noise and chaos level dramatically. Eventually, it became difficult for all of us to get together. The community was real, but it got harder to keep those bonds strong because of the nature of life and family. We started meeting less often, and our times together were more about corralling children than having heart-to-heart talks as adults.

One day, during that time period, I was on a walk with Eric Thomas, the guy who called to encourage me when Yvette was gone. Since that call, we had become friends. It turned out he had a house nearby, and we'd often meet up at six a.m. and walk together. I'd listen to him talk, and I'd learn as much as I could from him. His kids were several years older than mine, so as we walked that particular day, I asked him what I could expect in the coming years. He said, "I can't tell you what's coming up. It's impossible for me to know what speed bumps are ahead for you. But I know one thing that has always kept me: guarding my sacred circle."

Then he explained that often there's a group of men that you think you're going to age out of, or you may feel like you're not kicking it with them as much as you used to because you're not making time for them. "Don't forsake those men," he told me. "Keep that group. That's your sacred circle."

Right then, I decided to start meeting with the guys on a weekly basis. I reached out to all of them and said, "Hey, I talked to E. T., and I want to make sure we're intentional about our relationships. Can we get together every Wednesday?"

They all jumped in. We decided to make our guys' group a priority, and we never looked back. It became a place where we could talk and lift each other up. I've always been someone who talks about how I feel, but a lot of guys didn't have that access, so they ran to it.

I encourage you to take E. T.'s advice too: Build and guard a sacred circle. We all need a community of fathers around us. The Bible says, "As iron sharpens iron, so one person sharpens another" (Proverbs 27:17). I think men are good at sharpening each other on the basketball court or maybe in church, but when it comes to fatherhood, we're often on our own. It's not second nature for us to say, "I need a community of dads to rock with." For that to become our reality, we have to choose it.

CHOOSE YOUR CIRCLE

A while back, I was hanging out with one of the men in my community, a close friend named Karega whom I've known for years. He and his wife had just had a baby, and I was holding his newborn son and rocking him to sleep. Karega just stared at me for a minute, a strange look on his face, then said, "I never imagined another man holding my baby." It's not weird at all for women to hold each other's kids, but for men to do so wasn't something he had really seen before, and it was beautiful.

That moment meant a lot to both of us because it spoke to the bond we share. He told me, "As men, there's a belief that we have to lead our families and do it by ourselves. But I've seen so many examples of motherhood where women support each other by holding each other's babies and taking care of them, as well as by showing up for each other postpartum as their kids get older. I'm so blessed to know this type of bond with you."

He was saying that men don't get to enjoy that fatherhood bond enough—and he's right. Part of the problem is that our culture elevates and celebrates strong, individualistic men but subtly discounts or even makes fun of men who are tender and nurturing. But another part of the problem is within us; because we don't expect such a bond or believe for it, we don't pursue it. Most of us have never seen a fatherhood community in action, so we aren't doing enough to build or protect our sacred circle.

I'm convinced that needs to change. Fatherhood is too crazy, too hard, and too unpredictable for us to go at it alone. Somewhere along the line, we're going to find ourselves free-falling—headed for a breakdown or a bad decision—and we'll need someone to catch us, to hold us, to encourage us.

In a previous chapter I compared fatherhood to juggling. Sometimes, though, we need someone to catch *us*. We can't do all the holding, carrying, and lifting on our own. At moments, we all need someone who can pick us up with their encouragement, wisdom, friendship, advice, laughter, and embrace. I can't overstate the importance of this: *We need to be intentional about choosing and building our fatherhood community.* There is security and strength in having a larger network that can support us.

Along with Karega, I could recite a long list of men who mean the world to me, who have changed my life, who have caught me when I was falling, and who have challenged me and lifted me up. One of those men is Scotty James. When my wife asked, "What's your five-year plan?" and then fell asleep while I had an existential crisis for half the night, Scotty was the guy I sought out. His advice and coaching directly led to Beleaf in Fatherhood.

Kevin Fredericks, better known as KevOnStage, is a close friend who has carried me several times. I was on set with him filming a commercial when my youngest son was born early. Because of the unexpected timing, I missed the birth, and it crushed me. KevOnStage just hugged me, encouraged me, and told me I wasn't a bad father.

Another man in the group is Xavier Leon. One time when I needed to pay $8,000 in rent for my studio and didn't have the cash, he loaned it to me. He said, "I need it back, but let me know what you need, bro." I paid him back forty-five days later. I couldn't believe he'd trust me and help me like that. It meant the world to me.

Another is a guy named Jimmy Figueroa. Jimmy and I became friends before our wives knew each other. When I met his wife, she asked me, "Can we all hang out and be friends?" I said, "I don't do that. I don't pick my wife's friends. You meet her, and you guys figure it out." They ended up hitting it off, and the four of us are close friends now.

Garrett is another dad in my community. I've actually known him since middle school. We reconnected after I moved back to Cali in 2005, and he showed me a prayer journal of his. He had been praying for me since we were in middle school, and I had no idea. He bought his mom's old house, and now sometimes my kids have sleepovers with his kids at the same house where I slept over twenty-five years ago.

I could go on and on. There's Christian Hurst. He is my wife's godbrother. He was from her original community of friends and family—her tribe, her village—and we adopted him in. Pat changed my life, as I've said, and so did Dr. Carson. Eric Thomas helped catch me and empower me during that time my wife was away. There are other guys like Ray Castro, Timothy Jackson, and Jefferson Bethke. I wish I could take a page to honor what each one of these men has added to my life, but here's my point: I couldn't be the father I am without this community. I need them, and they need me.

In the same way, you need other men, and other men need you. This is true throughout life, but it's especially true as fathers.

YOU NEED OTHER MEN, AND OTHER MEN NEED YOU.

Who is in your sacred circle? Can you name them? Are you spending time with them? Are you guarding that sacred circle? If not, what could you do to begin building a stronger community?

This is not a critique in any way but rather a call to value the men around us. It's so easy to think we're doing just fine, we're being strong, we've got this covered. But inside, we might be falling, and we need someone to come alongside us.

It's funny because when my kids were young, I didn't know they'd need hugs when they got older. I thought when they turned five, that day would be over. Now they're nine, ten, eleven years old, and they still want to hug and cuddle. I'm turning forty soon, and I'm realizing more than ever how much *I* need to be hugged. As vulnerable as that sounds, when I'm weak, I need to be held by someone who is stronger than me. We never outgrow that, apparently. That's why we've got to make sure we're surrounding ourselves with people who can hold and support us.

Often when a friend and I meet up and give each other a hug, that's when I realize how much I needed to be hugged right then. I'm strong on the outside, but inside, I'm thinking, *Nah, I needed this.* They don't just hug me; they see me. They know what I'm carrying because they're carrying it too. We've all got money problems, family problems, and work problems, and it's so powerful to feel caught and held. It's like that scene from the movie *300* when the soldiers hold their shields together, forming a tight, impenetrable covering that protects them all.

A fatherhood community doesn't replace your connection with your wife and kids; instead, it supports it. Sometimes you need help from someone who is outside your immediate family—especially if it's your immediate family that is causing your current frustration or pain. I can talk with my wife about everything, but I also know I can't just dump on her all the time. I can't unload my frustrations on my kids. I need fathers I can turn to who will listen to me from a place of empathy, understanding, and bonding.

What I'm hoping for—not just for me, but for you and for fathers everywhere—is a community of men who really care about each other. Men who will say, "Hey, man, I love you," and really mean it. Men who understand that support and bonding isn't just for moms but for dads too, and we actually have access to it if we're willing to reach out.

CATCH, HOLD, UPLIFT

I'm not a juggler, but I know there are three stages to the process: First, you catch a ball that is falling, then you hold it until it's time to let it go, and finally you throw it upward. Then you do it all again, and again, and again.

When I think about how the men around me have helped me, I see the same three stages. As you're building a fatherhood community, you need people who can *catch*, *hold*, and *uplift* you. While the same people don't necessarily do all three things, if you have a big enough community of dads to rely on, you'll have the help you need.

1. CATCH

This is about getting help when you're falling. If you're spiraling downward emotionally, mentally, or in some other area, you need someone who can put out their hands and break your fall. I see this as an active, almost urgent intervention, when someone in your community halts you from going to a dark place or making a bad decision.

For someone to catch you, they need permission to step into your business. You can't expect people to know you need help if you don't tell them what's going on. If you feel like you're falling in some area right now, who could you go to for help? Who do you respect? Who is ahead of you in the fatherhood journey? Who has gone through something similar to what you're experiencing?

Eric Thomas caught me when I was in a dark place. He reached out to me while my wife was gone, which I didn't expect; but I was also reaching out for help when I spoke to his employee. I think that's how it often works. We don't know where help will come from, but if we start looking and asking, God will bring the person we need.

A catcher has to be empathetic and compassionate, but they also have to be strong. They need to be able to say, "This is not who you are, man. This is not what you want to do. You're bigger than this issue, and you're going to be okay." When I think back to the times other men have caught me, they were able to show me love and grace, but they also called me out on my mistakes or wrong attitudes. That takes courageous love. The Bible calls it "speaking the truth in love" (Ephesians 4:15). Someone who catches you will tell you what you need to hear, but they'll do it out of genuine love and concern for you. They'll help you, not shame you.

While you're thinking about who catches you, ask yourself the opposite question: Who are you catching? Are people around you falling, but they don't have the courage or knowledge to ask for help? Or maybe they are asking for help, but it's in their own way, and you need to hear their cry, step into their world, and speak truth in love. You might be the person who will change the trajectory of their life.

2. HOLD

I remember a time when some friends of ours came over to our house. They had been going through a chaotic season for a long time, and they were kind of beat up. Thanks to our four kids, the house was a mess. Even worse, something was wrong with our water system, so the tap water was brown and gross.

They didn't care at all. They just needed to be held. Not literally—although we hugged them when they came in—but emotionally. Immediately, their kids ran to the back of the house and started playing Nintendo Switch with our kids. While I made shrimp and grits, the parents cozied up and got glasses of wine, and we just kicked it. After the meal, I remember them saying they didn't want to leave. They were exhausted, and we had made them feel welcome. That was what they needed the most.

Sometimes my wife thinks she has to do a lot of stuff to make people feel welcome, like clean every nook and cranny. Sometimes I think I have to give amazing advice or fix people's problems. That isn't usually the case though. Often, people just need to be held.

Held is a protective, nurturing word. I've mentioned a few times how important it is for people to hold me when I feel weak, and that's what I'm talking about here. As fathers, this is especially important. People like KevOnStage have held me when I needed it desperately.

Do you have men in your life who are willing to hang on to you, to carry you, to embrace you, to protect you? I'm speaking both literally and figuratively here. Sometimes you need an actual hug, but beyond that, you need people who can carry you emotionally, spiritually, mentally. You need men who are willing to open themselves up when you are feeling weak and allow you to lean on their strength until you get through your battle.

For this to happen, you'll need to let yourself be held. We hear messaging all day, every day about how strong and independent we need to be as men, but that message is wrong. Sure, we need to be strong, but all our strength doesn't have to come from within; it should also come from the connections we have with others. And rather than being independent, lone-wolf fathers, we need to be interdependent, relying on one another and receiving from each other.

When you're being held, don't be in a hurry. In juggling, timing is everything, and if a ball is thrown too soon, it can mess everything up. Let yourself be held for as long as you need to be. Sooner or later you'll get back in the fight, but for now, there's no rush—and there's no shame in taking the time you need to be held.

Holding is for healing. Your family needs you at 100 percent, just as you need your spouse to be healthy and the Bulls needed Michael Jordan. Sometimes as dads, we're so focused on the health and well-being of our families that we neglect our own needs. That's not what our families want or deserve though. They need us to be the best possible versions of ourselves.

Letting yourself be held and healed is part of fathering yourself. In effect, we're fathering each other. Maybe we didn't have the most functional upbringing, and maybe we've carried some of that into the current versions of ourselves, but our story is still being written. The wounds and gaps we have from our childhood can be healed by the other men God brings into our lives. How beautiful is that? How powerful is that?

Therapy is a form of being held. I'm not saying you need to go to therapy, and I realize it can get expensive. But it's also an investment in your health. For me, it's been a way to be upheld by someone who knows more than I do about emotions, trauma, and the human brain, and it's helped me to unpack some of the luggage I carried for so long. As a result, I've found greater health and freedom to be the dad I need to be.

Find the "holders" in your life. Look for people who are patient, who see the potential in you, who love you sincerely, and who will give you the space and time you need without adding shame or guilt. At the same time, be willing to hold other people. At times you will be strong and healthy while someone near you is going through hell. How you react in those moments can change everything for that person. You don't need all the answers; just wrap your arms around them—literally or metaphorically—and be there for them for as long as they need your strength.

3. UPLIFT

Finally, there are men who know how to get you back in the game. While it's normal to fall from time to time, and while you need to be held while you heal, ultimately you were created to rise, soar, and fly. God's grace is enough for you. Even in the darkest times, you can know you will rise again.

You don't have to pick yourself up by your bootstraps. So often we want to fall alone, heal alone, and get back up alone, but that's not how life is meant to work. If you have a fatherhood community around you, they'll get you back on your feet and into play a lot faster. I love this passage from the Bible:

> Two are better than one,
> > because they have a good return for their labor:
> If either of them falls down,
> > one can help the other up.
> But pity anyone who falls
> > and has no one to help them up.
> Also, if two lie down together, they will keep warm.
> > But how can one keep warm alone?
> Though one may be overpowered,
> > two can defend themselves.
> A cord of three strands is not quickly broken.
>
> > (ECCLESIASTES 4:9–12)

For me, Scotty James is a good example of uplifting. He's the kind of guy who challenges me, asks hard questions, and calls me out on stuff. That day when we were discussing my five-year and fifteen-year plan, he didn't let me off the hook easily. He kept asking, "What if that doesn't work out? What are you going to do? Is that actually a good idea?" It almost felt rude and invasive, but I knew he was looking out for my best interests, so I stayed with the conversation, and I'm so glad I did. I walked out of his office realizing that in fifteen years, I didn't want to be rapping—I wanted to be telling people how great it is to be a father. And that's where I am today.

Who uplifts you when you need to be inspired, challenged, or encouraged? Think about people who can give you counsel or advice, who can see the potential in you and call it out of you, who can help you get past your excuses and step into your calling. These men are gold. They might get under your skin a little, but if they truly love you, they can be gifts from God to lead you higher and higher.

Of course, encouragement is a two-way street, and some men in your life will also need you to lift them up. Be the kind of father who sees the potential in other men and helps them get their head in the game. Never underestimate the power of an encouraging word. You don't know what all they're facing, and you don't know how hungry they are for someone to believe in them. Your faith in them can shift the way they see themselves—which will change everything for them.

BE THE KIND OF FATHER WHO SEES THE POTENTIAL IN OTHER MEN AND HELPS THEM GET THEIR HEAD IN THE GAME.

HOW TO BUILD A FATHERHOOD COMMUNITY

Years ago, a specific moment made me realize my friend group wasn't helping me grow. They weren't bad people, but they weren't going where I wanted to go. They didn't share my values, and they weren't building what I wanted to build in my family. I realized I needed to choose friends who thought higher, who would challenge me and sharpen me.

I've already shared some of the process I followed to surround myself with other fathers, and I described how Yvette and I have been intentional about connecting with families who are like-minded. You might be wondering how to do this for yourself though. It's one thing to recognize a need for a fatherhood community, but how do you make a community happen? Let me share a few final thoughts.

1. GOD BUILDS FAMILIES AND COMMUNITIES.

There's a verse in the book of Psalms that says, "God sets the lonely in families" (68:6). I believe that if you truly desire to be part of a family and a community, God will fulfill that desire.

When I think back over my own life, I can see it was God who brought people like Dr. Carson into my world. In a moment, we'll talk about some things you can do, but it's important to start by acknowledging how God wants this for you even more than you want it. He created you to be connected to other people. If you need a community, start by praying about it. Believe that God will bring the right men around you. He knows you need them, and he knows they need you.

2. AVAILABILITY AND VULNERABILITY ARE KEY.

While God will drop some people into your life out of sheer grace, there are other relationships you'll need to seek out. I'm not talking about faking or forcing anything here but simply making yourself available.

Pat is that kind of relationship for me. He gave me access to his home and family when I was in my early twenties and he was in his early thirties. I asked him recently why he trusted me and what he saw in me, and he said it came down to my hunger and my availability. He told me he could see that I wanted to learn and grow, and he was happy to help. That relationship was what gave me courage to have a family of my own.

Who could you reach out to? How could you make yourself more available? Who do you want to learn from? You can't force friendship any more than you can force a tree to grow, but you can provide an optimal environment for it to happen. You'll probably find that many other guys are just as hungry as you are for friendship and community. Often we're all just waiting for someone else to make the first move . . . so make the first move!

Vulnerability goes hand in hand with availability. If we say we want to have friends but we're not willing to let down our guard and allow other people in, nothing is going to change. We need to *need* friends. It's not easy to open up, but the rewards are worth the risk.

Vulnerability can't happen without safety. A lot of us have learned the hard way that when we let down our guards, people can take advantage of us. We must consciously override that safety mechanism if we're going to develop a real fatherhood community. There are people out there who will be a safe place for us, and we'll be a safe place for them. If we can find those people and invest in those relationships, we'll be able to let down our guards, open our hearts, and find the strength that comes from community.

3. GUARD YOUR CIRCLE.

I already talked about this, but it bears emphasizing: We must protect and invest in our friendships. Time marches on. Kids grow up. Schedules fill up. People move to new homes, get new jobs, and have new pressures. Don't let all those things crowd out the community you need. Some of your friendships will change, and some connections were meant only for a season, but don't drift away from relationships God wants to last a lifetime.

In our new home miles outside of the city, this has been a challenge for me. I'm in the process right now of figuring out what a community will look like. It takes more work, more time, and more gas money to get together with other families and other men, but I know it's worth it. Being part of a community that values what we value and supports and protects each other is a blessing worth fighting for.

"Guarding your circle" means investing in your relationships, but it *doesn't* mean closing yourself off to new relationships. Actually, the opposite is true: We should continually be expanding our communities and our circles of connections. Why? Because we have more to learn.

I need more evidence of good fatherhood. I need more skills, strategies, and knowledge. My kids are still young, and the more I discover about fatherhood, the more I realize how much I have left to learn. I'm trying to find more Pats and Dr. Carsons everywhere. I need more men around me, not fewer, as time moves on.

How about you? Who is in your sacred circle right now? Who else do you need to learn from? Who do you need to inspire and give access to? Who in your life could help you father yourself and become the parent your kids need? Maybe you need to call up a few guys and set up a weekly meeting. Maybe you need to get some dates on the calendar when you can just hang out and catch up with old friends.

The families you surround yourself with will create a ripple effect that continues generation after generation. That's why it's so important to build and guard your sacred circle. Yes, you should father yourself, but don't do it alone. Pull other fathers and families into your community and your circle. Together, we can show the world how beautiful fatherhood can be.

THANK YOU

Fatherhood is a blessing. You can call it a lot of other things too, but ultimately, it's a gift from God, and I'm so grateful for it. My heart's desire is that you would see it the same way.

I dream of a worldwide movement of men who fully embrace their roles as fathers. I dream of fathers who are willing to be open and vulnerable, to break stereotypes, to be proof of fatherhood, and to give access to other people so the narrative around fatherhood will change. That's not an impossible dream. I'm sure of it, and in a small way I'm proof of it, because my own fatherhood is the result of the many people who have invested in my life.

If you are a father, I hope you can see the value you add to your family. Please know they are better because you are there. No, you won't be perfect, but that's okay. That's what family is for, after all: to hold each other up in times of need.

You are seen, you are needed, and you are valued. Thank you for all you do. Keep fathering yourself, and you'll be the dad your kids need and deserve.

ACKNOWLEDGMENTS

Start

Thank you, Father God! I can't believe that you have been so generous with me, showing all the parallels between you and me and my kids and me. I sit in silence during these revelations, just gratefully drawn to worship you. Thank you for holding me. All I ever need is your embrace.

Yvette, we've been really doing the work. This author season has taught us both, and one thing that has been obvious is that we don't have to hide our trauma from each other. We can fall apart within our marriage and embrace the complicated undoing of what we thought had molded us. You are a true treasure. This partnership has been the joy of my life, and I can't wait for the coauthor work we are embarking on.

Theophilus, God gave you the gift of awareness, and you have been looking out for all of us since you could make gestures. But you're capable of more than just the physical feats you excel in. Your presence alone birthed a posture of accountability in me that no grown man could hold me to; you're powerful.

Uriah Beau, I already know you're smiling reading this—you can't help it, and that's what makes you special. You've taught me to find the joy in all things because of how pure you are. This was one of my hardest lessons because of my own childhood experience, but you are helping heal that part of me.

Anaya Zai, there is a moment when every father meets his match, and it's truly when he first lays eyes on his daughter. Most men think they are going to become softer if they embrace quality time with their daughters. You've taught me that the softness is necessary for real growth.

Uzi, your birth brought the family together in a special way. You've taught me to cherish the moments of rest and restoration.

Dad, letting me move to California and start over was the catalyst to me knowing the Lord, becoming an emcee, finding my wife, and becoming a father. I'm grateful for the time we spend together. Talks in the garage have proved to be therapeutic for both of us. Love you!

Mike Salisbury, I can't even put into words how much your love and care has helped me reconstruct my inner voice. Your grace and patience are in alignment with our calling as believers. Thank you for being the standard for agencies in the book industry.

Karen Yates, your expertise and knowledge of the book industry is top-tier. I'm grateful to have access to your knowledge, and I appreciate the way you delicately guide me through this journey.

To my collaborator, Justin Jaquith: Other than my wife and therapist you probably know me the deepest. We really weaved through a good amount of past trauma to dig out the gold. Thank you!

To my editor, Hanha Parham: You supported my ideas with curiosity and gave me a lot of hope while I was roughing it on the farm. Thank you!

To my graphic designer, RJ: You were my first collaborator for Beleaf in Fatherhood. Your creativity is woven into the fabric of this brand, and you killed the cover!

I have much appreciation for the collaborators and supporters of this book. There are so many more people working behind the scenes, so I want to say a general thank-you for their commitment to telling great stories. To my Yates & Yates team, my Thomas Nelson team, and my Kensington Grey team, thank you for your care on this journey.

ABOUT THE AUTHOR

Author

len Henry, the creative force behind the immensely popular YouTube channel Beleaf in Fatherhood, is a visionary content creator, devoted father, and beacon of inspiration for parents worldwide. Beyond his YouTube channel, Glen is an advocate for positive parenting and family values, actively engaging with his audience through social media platforms, workshops, and speaking engagements. His dedication to promoting healthy relationships between fathers and their children has made him a sought-after voice in the parenting sphere.